10p

D1327917

Investment

COLLINS NUTSHELL BOOKS

Investment

RUSSELL TAYLOR

COLLINS
LONDON AND GLASGOW

First published 1963
Revised edition 1970

Contents

1

STOCKS AND SHARES

Some years ago you were left some money. Say it was
£400 in 1951. Instead of spending it you decided to save it.
You probably decided to be "safe" and bought a government stock. $2\frac{1}{2}$% Consols, one of the favourite methods of
saving for the small investor, cost £66 for £100 nominal of
stock in 1951. It gave a return of £3 15s. for every £100
invested. You would still be getting that £3 15s. but the
price of the stock is now a little less than £30. In other
words, your savings would have lost well over half of
their capital value and, of course, the £3 15s. interest no
longer buys as much as it did because of inflation. You
might have deposited it with a building society. £400
placed with them would have brought you an income of
£2 5s. per £100 or £9 a year tax paid and your savings
would have been absolutely safe: furthermore they could
have been withdrawn without loss at any time during
those years. By now the income would have risen to
£5 10s. per £100 and the £400 would still be there. Unfortunately prices of nearly all goods have risen during
those intervening years. That £400 would buy only £300
worth of goods to-day. Perhaps you chose to use the
money as the down payment on a house. You would
have had an income from this, either rent-free living for
yourself or rents from tenants, but the capital could only
have been realised as cash by selling the house. This
might have been difficult and it is possible you would
have received less for the house than you paid for it. If
this did happen, you would have been unlucky, for, on
average, house prices have increased by over 400 per cent

since 1950: in particularly favourable areas they have risen even even further.

It is also possible that you were very daring and bought some shares on the Stock Exchange. Fifty £1 Ordinary shares of Schweppes, the soft drinks people, at 70s. a share—the highest price in 1951—would have cost £175. Five times during the next few years the company raised more money for expansion by offering shares on favourable terms to existing shareholders. These "rights" could have been sold, some sold so that the remainder of the shares allotted could be paid for from the proceeds, or all could have been taken up. This last would have cost another £307. If you had needed the money urgently during these years and you had had to sell the shares suddenly, it is conceivable that you would have received less for them than you paid: the income from the shares, which is paid out of profits and called the dividend, might have ceased if the company had done badly. Neither happened. The company prospered and the income on the original investment would have risen from £7 10s. a year before tax to approximately £100 to-day. The 50 £1 shares, what with "rights" and "free" issues and the merger with Cadburys, have become 2,612 5s. shares. At the 1969 price of 17s.* your savings of £482 (£175 plus £307) would have grown to £2,220. Of course you might have chosen a company which did badly—and then you could have lost everything.

Ways to Save
Most of us save, however little it may be. All of us want to

* This was the latest available price. Since then this price, like all others given in this book, has changed. Fictitious companies could have been used instead of real ones and then there would have been no such problem. But the actual prices given are not important—they are merely illustrations for the argument. Since this is so, it is much better that real companies, and real shares with their prices, should be used. It is these that you will be dealing with when you come to invest.

ensure that our savings will be adequate for our needs and, we would prefer, a little more than adequate. But although economic conditions have changed beyond recognition since before the war, our saving habits have not kept up with these changes.

There are two main ways of saving: saving by acquiring financial assets or real assets. The best-known way of acquiring financial assets is by opening deposit accounts with reputable building societies, savings banks or the Post Office, or by buying National Saving Certificates or Development Bonds. The money is safe, can be withdrawn without any loss any time it is wanted and offers a secure yearly income. * It is ideal as a method of short-term saving for it enables a reserve of money to be kept for emergencies. Then there are British Government stocks. These have different names but they all have one thing in common. Their interest payments are guaranteed by the British government. Some of these stocks are dated— that is, the Government will repay them at par, £100 for £100 nominal of stock on some specified date—others are undated. Nevertheless, all these are really long-term methods of saving, for the market prices of these stocks are always being affected by political and economic considerations. Another popular method of long-term saving is to take out an endowment policy with a life assurance company. This does not give any income on the money invested but instead pays out at the end of a stated period rather more than has been paid in. This is not good as a method of short-term saving as these savings cannot easily be turned into cash.

None of these methods solves the basic problem of

* This is not true of National Saving Certificates which offer a tax free capital profit at the end of a specified period instead. But sufficient certificates can be sold every year to give a yearly income while retaining the original capital value of the savings.

keeping up with inflation—that is, the rise in the price of goods. There is no point in scrimping and saving for retirement if at the end of it all the savings have depreciated so much that they are useless.

The way many of us save by acquiring real assets is by buying a house. The structure itself is fairly permanent; the land on which it stands is scarce and everlasting. If prices rise, house values can also be expected to rise. The other way of acquiring real assets is by purchasing a share in a business. Most people can do this only by buying shares on the Stock Exchange. That the Stock Exchange, to so many people the synonym of speculation, should be a centre for saving may seem odd. Yet the industrial shares bought and sold there are exactly what their name implies. There are 215,436,000 Marks & Spencer shares in issue at the time of writing; the owner of 100 M. & S. shares is the owner of a $\frac{100}{215,436,000}$th worth of all Marks & Spencer's shops, stocks and trade connections as well as of the ability and loyalty of the directors and staff. When prices rise, the value of M. & S. shops and stocks will obviously rise as well. If all prices rise, then M. & S. can raise its own prices. If prices are rising, then the company should succeed in making bigger profits every year—even if all that these higher profits really mean is that the same number of goods were sold as in the previous year but at a higher price. Because profits rise, the company is able to pay larger dividends to its shareholders; then more people want to buy the shares and so the share price also rises. This is why Ordinary shares are said to be "hedges against inflation." They do not stop it but they do keep up with it. There are two important provisos to this. It applies only to well-run firms, and only to the Ordinary shares—not the Preference.

10

Why Ordinary Shares Became Popular

The popularity of Ordinary shares as a means of saving is
still fairly new. Before the war the Church Commissioners,
the insurance companies, the pension funds of large firms
and local authorities and the building societies would never
have dreamt of investing in anything but the very best
fixed interest securities. They went for security of capital
and certainty of income. Their attitude changed for two
reasons. One was the teaching of a great British economist
called John Maynard Keynes and the other the signing of
the Atlantic Charter in 1944 by the countries of the
Western Alliance.

The advance of the world's material prosperity has never
been a steady upward movement but a series of cycles—
"booms" followed by "busts." But in the "bust" times
factories would close their gates, millions of people would
be thrown out of work and even the strongest companies
suffered terribly and had to pass (that is, fail to pay) their
dividends. Many of the smaller companies went bankrupt.
As a result Ordinary shares were not at all popular with
savers. Keynes did not succeed in solving the problem of
the "business cycle"—indeed no one has yet explained
this satisfactorily—but he did show how governments
could moderate their violence and, in particular, avoid the
devastating slumps that had been a feature of all capitalist
economies up to that time. In the Atlantic Charter the
countries of the west agreed to follow these Keynesian
economic policies and thus maintain full employment.
The business cycle is still with us and it does mean that
some years will be much more profitable for companies
than others—but there is now no reason at all why a
sound and well-managed company should not substantially increase both its profits and its dividends over a
period of years. There is certainly no reason for it to pass
its dividend or to go bankrupt. Not all companies will do

as well as Schweppes or Marks & Spencer, but they should do well. The value of the shares of the thirty staid companies that make up the *Financial Times* Index of Ordinary Shares have more than quadrupled since 1950—the income from them has more than doubled.

Policies of full employment have brought in an unexpected by-product—rising prices or inflation. Many people get extremely upset about the evils of inflation. This can be understood when it is remembered that in the 1930s you could expect your pound to buy more goods every year, not less. But the obverse to this happy picture was three million unemployed and the misery of all industrial Britain—and this completely precludes the tremendous loss of national wealth caused by the unemployment of so many men, machines and factories. Inflation has appeared not only in Britain but in every industrialised country, and many economists feel that not only is the mild type of inflation which we know in England harmless (provided that there are certain safeguards, such as the adjustment of pensions for those living on fixed incomes), but that it is also a necessary adjunct to a full employment society. There is no question that a sane government will recreate the conditions of the 1930s, and savers would be well advised to stop railing against inflation and to try to beat it instead.

Virtually all the large financial institutions had realised by the early 1950s that greater economic stability together with inflation made the buying of Ordinary shares both desirable and necessary. Many private trustees would also have liked to buy Ordinary shares but were legally unable to do so. Legislation was finally passed in 1961 allowing trustees to place 50% of the funds they administer into selected Ordinary shares. Now it is only the private saver who has no means of protecting himself against inflation.

What is the Stock Exchange?

The most newsworthy items about the Stock Exchange—
take-over battles and bankruptcies, and the tremendous
rises and falls in share prices associated with them—are
those that are least typical. The enormous sums of
money raised by industry every year for research and expansion and the great number of introductions of new
companies to the stock market, some of which will become the nationally known businesses of the future, are
rarely mentioned. The Stock Exchange itself has been
remarkably coy about publicising its activities and so it is
no surprise that most people, with garbled history book
tales of the South Sea Bubble and the Wall Street crash,
still regard it as a gambling casino. Of course, there are
sharp-fingered speculators in the Stock Exchange as there
are in all markets—that is all that the Stock Exchange is,
a market, but one that deals in loans instead of cars or
cabbages.

The best-known part of the Stock Exchange is the
industrial share market. This has become really important
only since the First World War and the majority of stock
exchange transactions are still concerned with the buying
and selling of the loans of government and public authorities. In the last century businesses were built up on the
private fortunes of the owners and their friends. Taxation
and death duties have reduced both the number and size
of private fortunes while the increasing complexity of
industrial processes makes the financial demands of most
companies much greater than could be supplied by private
individuals, however rich. Businesses have to call upon
strangers for their "risk" or "equity" capital instead.
Strangers, unlike family and friends, are not willing to
lend money for ever; they are prepared to lend only if
they can get their money back whenever they want. The
Stock Exchange is the meeting place where businesses can

find individuals prepared to put up money for their enterprises and where shareholders who wish to sell can find others prepared to buy. Furthermore, since trading goes on continuously, firms can easily tell how much their new borrowing will cost them and individuals can always know how much their shareholdings are worth.

Is Buying Shares a Useful Function?

Much of the trading in shares is between private individuals. Because of this many people doubt whether buying shares is lending money to industry at all. It is perfectly true that when you buy 100 Imperial Chemical Industries (ICI) shares you probably find that you are buying them from a Mrs. Brown or a Mr. Smith. It may also be true that the money Mrs. Brown gets for her shares is earmarked for a fur coat or a holiday in the South of France. That is certainly not lending money to ICI. But unless everyone can sell his shares whenever he wants and for whatever purpose he wants, no one would be prepared to buy shares at all. Industry has raised £300 million a year on average since the war for research and expansion. Much of this has come from new money that the institutions are always collecting—new insurance premiums for instance—and which they immediately invest. But a great deal has come from private shareholders—reinvestment of dividends or new savings. Mrs. Brown might easily be selling her ICI to take up "rights" shares offered to her by another of the companies in which she is a shareholder or to apply for the shares of a new company coming to the market for the first time.

Risks of Ordinary Shares

Ordinary shares are a much safer investment than they used to be but there are still risks attached to them, in particular, certain risks which the new investor should never forget.

The price of a share depends on public confidence in the company, the industry of which it is a part, the government's economic policy and the internal and external political situation. The long-term trend of a share price may be upwards, but fears about the economy or the possibility of war can lead to a heavy fall. Such falls can never be foretold. Buying Ordinary shares is long-term saving. Buying Ordinary shares without a cash reserve for emergencies is begging to lose money. This cannot be repeated too often. Anyone contemplating buying Ordinary shares, however rich, should have a reserve of savings which can easily be realised as cash. This normally means a deposit with a bank or building society. Many City people also feel that no one should buy shares before they have a house and life insurance. The first is debatable. The second is not. You may intend to save £100 a year by buying shares. If you die shortly after your first investment, £100 will not be of much use to your family. Life insurance gives complete and immediate cover as soon as the first instalment is paid. Furthermore, some life insurance schemes give protection against inflation. These are the "with profits" endowment policies. The usual sort of endowment policy involves paying premiums for a certain number of years, perhaps £100 a year for 20 years. At the end of 20 years you either get a lump sum of about £2,000 or some sort of yearly income. If you die before the 20 years are up your family gets the money. However, because of inflation £2,000 may not be nearly so attractive in 20 years' time as it is to-day. The answer to this is the "with profits" policy. A slightly higher premium is paid and the £2,000 still awaits you at the end of 20 years but, in addition, you will share in the profits that the insurance company makes when it invests the money you pay as premiums. These depend on the company's success in investing its funds on the Stock Exchange and attracting new customers for its policies. Since both the Conservative and Labour parties are committed to increasing our national wealth, the insurance companies should continue to do well on both counts. At present rates a "with profits" policy for £2,000 could earn an extra £1,500 at the end of 20 years. That should be sufficient to offset any likely price rise.

The other risk concerns the company. Profits are affected not only by the ups and downs of the business cycle but also by technological change, which can make a company's products obsolete and unwanted, competition from other firms or other countries, which can cut down profit margins, or plain bad management. These factors can cause company profits to fall very sharply; in bad years dividends could be cut or passed. The share price falls and the investor loses income and capital. Misfortune can hit suddenly and without warning at the most respected companies in the most prosperous industries. In 1960, hire purchase companies produced appallingly bad results against most people's expectations; some companies went bankrupt and all investors lost heavily. This very real risk can be minimised by spreading investments and never having more than a small percentage of your savings in any one industry.

2

WHAT'S WHAT ON THE STOCK EXCHANGE

There are over 10,000 different securities quoted on the London Stock Exchange, and although you may be interested only in growth equities it is important to know the characteristics of these other securities. These 10,000 securities can be split two ways: either between fixed interest and variable interest stocks or between public authority and company securities.

The Funds

This is the most important and by far the largest market. It is also called the "gilt-edged" or "Consols" market and comprises all British Government stocks such as Consols $2\frac{1}{2}\%$, Conversion 5% 1971, or Treasury $2\frac{1}{2}\%$, and British Government guaranteed securities, such as British Transport 3% 1968-73, or British Gas 4% 1969-72.

The Others

There are many other fixed interest stocks of this type. Corporation and County stocks offer slightly higher yields than British Government stocks but, though quite as safe since, in the last resort, their credit is that of the government, they are not so easily marketable. There is also the stock issued by public boards—Harbour & Dock Boards, some Water Boards, etc.—and Dominion and Colonial Government stocks as well as stock issued by provinces or corporations within these countries. Some of these are trustee stocks—that is, they are available for purchase by private trustees. But most of them are much less marketable than British funds and the slightly higher yield is generally not worth the extra risk. There are also stocks issued by foreign governments and corporations—many of these are "busted," that is, the Government which should be paying interest on them has defaulted, and they are often used as speculative stocks. These are stocks which should certainly not be bought by the average investor.

Differences

Stock issued by public authorities can either be dated, which means that at some particular time in the future the loan will be repaid either at par value or at some figure agreed when the original issue is made, or undated. These undated stocks are sometimes called "irredeemables" or "perpetuals." In fact, most of them are "one way options." The government can repay them at par if it wishes to, but has no legal obligation to do so. Such well-known stocks as Consols $2\frac{1}{2}\%$ (old Consols) or Treasury $2\frac{1}{2}\%$ (often referred to as Daltons in somewhat doubtful honour of the Chancellor of the Exchequer who issued them in a last vain attempt to keep money cheap after the war), War Loan and Conversion 3% all come into this category. The dated stocks can either be repaid at a specified date (for instance $4\frac{3}{4}\%$ Conversion, repaid or converted into another stock on the 15th June, 1963) or repaid during a period laid down at the time of the issue; the government, for instance, can repay 3% British Gas at any time between 1990 and 1995, but must repay it some time before the end of 1995. When it chooses to do so will depend on current interest rates. If the Government can make new borrowings more cheaply than the terms offered by the existing stock, then obviously it is advantageous to convert as soon as possible. Otherwise it will allow the issue to run its full life. These days this usually happens.

Yields

Stock is issued with a coupon. Consols $2\frac{1}{2}\%$ has a coupon of $2\frac{1}{2}$. In other words, for every £100 worth of stock the government will pay interest of £2 10s. Naturally, no one in present circumstances would be prepared to accept such a low return from his money, and so the price of the stock itself fluctuates. At the time of writing £100 nominal of Consols $2\frac{1}{2}\%$ can be bought for £26. This means that the actual return you are getting on your money is not £2 10s., but $\dfrac{\text{Nominal Value of stock} \times \text{Coupon}}{\text{Present Price.}}$ At the moment this is $\dfrac{100 \times 2\frac{1}{2}}{26}$ or a little over £9 10s. This is usually called the flat or running yield. The position is a little more complicated with dated stocks. This is because the yield that you are receiving on your money consists of the coupon yield, which is taxable, and a tax-free capital profit. This tax-free capital profit is the difference between how much you will get for the stock if you hold it to its redemption date and the amount that you pay for it now. At present British Transport 1978-88 costs £48 for £100 nominal and so the running yield is $\dfrac{100 \times 3}{48}$ or a return on your money of approximately £6 5s. However, by 1988 at the latest there will be a tax-free capital gain of £52. If this is spread over the life of the security and added to the coupon yield, the result is what is known as the "gross redemption yield." This particular sum cannot be worked out absolutely exactly, but, given certain assumptions, a fairly close approximation can be made. This is a very complicated sum, and since the *Financial Times* does it for you, there is little need to go into the theory. The gross redemption yield on British Transport 1978-88 at £48 is £8 12s. 9d. In fact, this is still not much use

19

in estimating what return you will get on your money since part of the return is taxable. For this reason brokers who specialise in gilt-edged securities also calculate—generally on computers—a "net redemption yield." This is a combination of the tax-free capital gain and the taxable running yield and is worked out with tax at 7s. 6d. in the £—for the benefit of life insurance companies who are taxed at this special rate—and at 8s. 3d. in the £ for everyone else. In this case the net redemption yield on Transport 1978-88 is £6 13s.

Payment of Interest

Interest on $2\frac{1}{2}\%$ Consols is paid quarterly—in January, April, July and October—but is paid half-yearly on all other stock. Generally it is paid "tax paid," but certain stocks are paid gross to non-residents. A short dated gilt—one which will be redeemed within five years—is dealt in "firm." That means that the buyer pays and the seller gets any accrued interest. Other gilts—medium dated which are between 5-15 years, long dated which are 15 years and over, and undated stocks—are dealt in "flat." The price is adjusted for any accrued interest. Dealings take place in multiples of 1d.; there is no stamp duty and brokers charge a very small commission on gilt-edged dealings. As a result the institutions can have fun switching from one stock to another to improve their income slightly. This, is not something for the small investor.

Attraction of Gilts

Gilts offer a secure yield because it is impossible to imagine the British Government defaulting on its obligations. Yet there is no security of capital; post-war inflation and a monetary policy which has consistently emphasised high interest rates have resulted in substantial falls in the book value of gilt-edged stocks. This is stale news to those who bought War Loan in 1950 at around £90 and now see them nearer £40. Yet the secure regularity of a gilt-edged dividend is essential to many portfolios and the proper choice of a dated stock is often the best answer to the problem of investing money which will be needed at a particular date.

More important to the average investor, the atmosphere of the gilt-edged market is indicative of the standing of the government's economic policies. It also shows the general level of confidence in the future of the £ sterling. Equity price movements generally discount economic recovery and rising industrial profits; the factors which allow industry to expand—easing of monetary restrictions and falling interest rates—are good for the gilt-edged market. There has rarely been a substantial equity bull market not supported by strong gilt-edged price movement and there seems no reason to suppose that equity and gilt-edged markets will not continue to move parallel in future— even though, since 1959, there has been a "reverse yield gap" with gilts yielding more than equities. A safe rule of thumb is that a strong equity market combined with a weak gilt-edged market is inherently suspicious.

Company Securities

A company can raise money by means of loans or by issuing share capital. Company loan capital is similar to government stock in many ways, except that virtually all of it is "dated" nowadays. Nevertheless a trading risk is involved with company loans. While governments are unlikely to go bankrupt, a company might.

This loan capital is generally described as a Debenture or loan stock.* There are many variants on these two names

---

* There are legal differences of no real importance to the investor between "stocks" and "shares." Suffice it to say that "stock" is nowadays used to refer to securities with a nominal value of £100 while "shares" refers to those securities with small nominal values— mainly the Preference and Ordinary share capital of companies.

but the essential difference is that Debentures are normally secured on some real asset belonging to the company while loan stock is normally unsecured. However, shareholders cannot be paid anything until the loan stock has been serviced, and this is as good a security as some piece of land or equipment which might, in the last resort, turn out to be unsaleable. Debentures offer a somewhat higher yield than government or corporation stocks and are a rather difficult market.

Institutions are large holders of Debenture and loan stock, and they ensure that companies are not able to pursue any form of borrowing policy that jeopardises the safety of existing Debenture or loan stock holders: the profits cover for Debentures and other prior charges can be seen from the "priority percentages" on the Exchange Telegraph card (*see* Chapter 5). Provided the company is of a reasonable size and fairly competently managed, this is a perfectly safe security offering a reasonable yield and the promise of repayment at a specified date in the future.

The Best of Both Worlds

Company loan stock suffers from the same disadvantage as does government stock and has become an expensive, and often difficult, way of raising money. This has resulted in the Convertible Debenture or loan stock. The company gets money on a fixed return basis, the investor an immediate high yield together with the opportunity of switching into the equity at a later date.

The issue by British Oxygen Company of a $7\frac{1}{2}\%$ Convertible Unsecured Loan Stock 1987/92 is an interesting example. The stock offers investors an immediate yield of $7\frac{1}{2}\%$. This compares with a dividend yield of $4\cdot5\%$ on the Ordinary shares. It attracts both those investors who want a high yield and those who think British Oxygen will do well in the future but would like to hedge their bets a little.

On 1st March 1970 this stock can be converted into Ordinary shares at the rate of 215 Ordinary shares for every £100 of loan stock. This values the Ordinary shares at about 9s. 3d. compared with their present price of 11s. 10d. In 1971 conversion is at 200 shares for £100 or a value of 10s. for every Ordinary share and in 1972 conversion is at 185 shares per £100 or a value of 10s. 9d. for every Ordinary share. This is also interesting from the point of view that the valuation of the shares on conversion is less than the current market price. For this reason there is a premium of 17% on the Loan Stock which means that every £100 of stock is currently costing £117. This reduces the immediate yield of $7\frac{1}{2}$% to 6·58% approximately.

Now if the company does well, profits rise and the dividend is increased; it follows that the value of the Ordinary shares will increase too and it will then be profitable to convert. If the company does badly, conversion will not be profitable. But the dividend on the Loan Stock will be quite safe and it will be repaid at par between 1987/92.

Preference Shares

Preference shares come in all sorts and shapes such as participating—a share in equity profits above a certain level, cumulative—arrears of Preference dividends accumulate and rank before any Ordinary dividends, non-cumulative—the opposite, redeemable and irredeemable. But the important thing is that a Preference shareholder is a shareholder. This means that he is liable to the full extent of his investment and no more in the company's fortunes or misfortunes; a Debenture holder lends his money to the company and is not involved in its business issue. His position is protected by law and if the company goes bankrupt he is at the head of the queue for repayment. A Preference shareholder is fully involved in all the company's business risks. If the company goes bankrupt he is at the back of the queue.

The Preference shareholder is entitled to a fixed dividend. If the company does well it is the Ordinary shareholder, not the Preference shareholder, who benefits. If the company does very badly the Preference shareholder may, as likely as not, lose his dividend and will suffer equally with the Ordinary shareholder. Quite often Preference shareholders have very restricted voting rights, or no votes at all, unless their dividends are in arrears; their general weakness in company affairs vis-a-vis other shareholders has resulted in their being treated rather unfairly by take-over bidders. And so the investment popularity of Preference shares—which offer a slightly better yield than Debentures of equivalent investment ranking—has been declining since the war.

Ordinary Shares

Everything that is left after all prior charges have been satisfied belongs to the Ordinary shareholder. The "residual" or "equity" of the company is difficult to measure and so no exact value can be put on an Ordinary share. But there is no doubt that while the Preference and Ordinary shareholders often have to take the rough together, it is the Ordinary shareholder that gets all the smooth. And in the conditions of the post-war world there has been much more smooth than rough. This accounts for the popularity of Ordinary shares.

3

HOW THE STOCK MARKET WORKS

The Stock Exchanges

When people talk of the Stock Exchange, they nearly always mean the London Stock Exchange. This is probably fair, because, although there are another 21 stock exchanges within the country, London is by far the biggest. However, most of the provincial stock exchanges have federated within recent years. The Midlands and West Stock Exchange now consists of the following former stock exchanges or "trading floors": Birmingham, Bristol, Cardiff, Nottingham and Swansea. The Northern Stock Exchange incorporates the following floors: Huddersfield, Leeds, Liverpool, Manchester, Newcastle-upon-Tyne, Oldham and Sheffield; while the Scottish Stock Exchange consists of Aberdeen, Dundee, Edinburgh and Glasgow. In addition, individual stock exchanges still exist in Belfast, Cork and Dublin, and the Provincial Brokers Stock Exchange incorporates individual brokers situated in offices throughout the country in towns without an established trading floor. All these Exchanges have their own list of stocks etc., etc. There is now talk of a future merger of all these exchanges into one national Stock Exchange.

Stockbrokers

For the last 300 years an unwary public has been suffering the consequences of its own gullibility. For about the same period of time the stockbroker has been receiving the blame. The fact that the stockbroker uses a technical jargon incomprehensible to most laymen, together with the wide fluctuations in share prices, has always combined to persuade most outsiders that the stockbroker is part of a diabolical combination designed to fleece anyone foolish enough to start investing. But the stockbroker's jargon is simply the technical language that any profession evolves, and the price movements are the result of the public's buying and selling; the stockbroker is simply the buying and selling agent of the public.

You cannot go to law without a lawyer; you will find it difficult to cure yourself without a doctor; you will not be able to buy shares without a stockbroker. This is where the difficulty for most people comes in, for stockbrokers, like lawyers and doctors, are professional men and cannot advertise. How are you to find a stockbroker and, having found one, will he accept your business?

Meeting a Stockbroker

The best way of getting a stockbroker is through the recommendation of a friend: for most people this is a counsel of perfection. Another way is to ask people, such as accountants, solicitors, or bankers, who can be expected to come across stockbrokers in the course of their professional duties, for an introduction. Failing this, it is an excellent idea to write to the Secretary of the London Stock Exchange—or of the local exchange if you prefer— and ask him to send a list of brokers who are prepared to take on new business. You can also write to the Secretary of the Provincial Brokers Stock Exchange at 3 Sampson Gate, York. This is not a stock exchange in the sense that London and Manchester are, but it is an organisation for brokers who do business in towns where there is no stock exchange. The Secretary of the PBSE will send you a complete list of members so that you will be able to see if there is a broker within your own town. Finally, you can always buy shares through your local bank manager. The bank itself should not give advice—beware of the bank manager who does—but they will certainly send on your queries to their own branch stockbroker and relay the answer to you. When you want to buy and sell, they will do it for you. The bank will share the stockbroker's commission so that there is no extra charge for this service.

The one way not to meet a stockbroker is by receiving a letter or personal visit from someone who will offer to buy or sell shares for you. Stockbrokers have a very strict code of behaviour which is designed to protect their clients. One of their rules is that they are not allowed to advertise or tout for business or act as principals. Anyone who does so is obviously not a member of a recognised Stock Exchange, so do not do business with such a person.

Will He Want Your Business?

The stockbroker's business is buying and selling shares for the public. His living comes from the commission that he makes. A £100 investment covers his direct clerical expenses; £500 probably makes him a profit. It is not fair to him to expect him to lose money by giving him very small amounts of money to invest. It is probably better for the small saver—and that means people with only about £100 at a time to put into Ordinary shares—either to buy through a bank or to buy unit trusts or to invest through an Investment Club. Fortunately, there are brokers who are interested in encouraging small savers to invest through the Stock Exchange and they are prepared to take on unprofitable business.

What Your Stockbroker Will Do For You

You may feel that the savings you already have, or your regular yearly savings, are sufficient to justify getting a stockbroker. Your stockbroker will certainly not make you a millionaire. He probably won't even make money for you consciously. That is not his job. His job is to buy and sell shares on your orders and, because he is a professional and has a great deal of experience, to advise you on the investment plan that will best suit your needs. He will also give you information on the shares you want to buy.

Your broker will not be able to give you intelligent advice on how best to invest your savings unless he knows your financial position. Make an appointment to see him and tell him what your assets are—whether you have a regular job, or are self-employed, whether you possess a house or life insurance, what savings you have. Tell him, too, what your liabilities are—whether you have a family to support, house payments to make, children to educate, or retirement to plan for. He will then be able to advise you whether you would do best in shares which give a good immediate return but will show little or no capital appreciation or in those that give a low immediate income but above-average prospects of capital appreciation. After deciding what type of investment policy to pursue—and most savers with a regular job should go for capital growth rather than income—he should then be able to advise you on shares. He can tell you such things as whether a share price is high because a lot of people are speculating on the company's results, whether the price is low because of a rights issue, or selling of stock after a take-over, whether it is suitable for the purpose you have in mind and countless other details. He might also advise you to stay clear of a particular company. If he does, follow his advice. The small unsound company, the price of which suddenly starts rising fantastically, has a fatal attraction for the small and unknowledgeable investor. All too often the shares of these companies are being manipulated by their directors or other large shareholders. When suddenly, overnight, the share price falls to zero, investors wonder what has happened. They have been taken for a ride. Too many small savers lose everything by ignoring the advice of their broker. This is speculation pure and simple and a game which never pays.

Local versus London

The London broker has the advantage of being in the country's largest market and this is an attraction which seems pre-eminent to most investors. Yet if you are interested in increasing your savings by buying growth stocks, you are going to have to be in close touch with your broker. Long letters are time consuming and unsatisfactory, and long distance telephone calls will soon eat up your profits. Furthermore, local brokers are very much closer to the companies in their area than London brokers can ever be and the opportunities for increasing your capital by investing in good local firms is every bit as good as by buying glamorous London "blue chips."

What is a Good Broker?

Making money on the Stock Exchange takes time. It involves continuous supervision of the shares in a portfolio and frequent consideration of which companies still appear capable of increasing their profits and dividends and which companies seem to have come to the end of their growth. This is your job, not your broker's. Even the management of a portfolio, which really only involves half-yearly valuations, the taking up of rights and scrip issues and the occasional weeding out of obviously unsuitable shares, is an expensive and time-consuming job. A recent letter to the *Financial Times* suggested that brokers found managing portfolios of £10,000 uneconomic. This may be rather an exaggeration as there are obviously

29

many brokers who would be delighted with a portfolio of £10,000. Nevertheless, although a stockbroker should not be expected to make you money, he should certainly prevent you from losing it. Naturally stockbrokers are no more omniscient than anyone else. They cannot be expected to forecast a slump in stock market prices because of a political crisis. But a good broker should be able, when asked, to advise on a company—its need for money and the likelihood of a rights issue, the pressure of competition and the trend of profit margins, its record and some enlightening, if libellous, comments on the quality of its management. If you are not satisfied with the advice and attention you get from your broker, don't blame the system, just find a new broker.

Price Quotations

Assume that you have found a broker and that you and he have decided that you should go for capital growth stocks. You mention something about motors or chemicals. He probably discourages you from buying many of the shares you immediately mention because he says that the industry is doing badly, or competition is expected to increase, or the company, though well known, has bad management. He suggests that you look at a company called Albright & Wilson. You will find it inside the back page of the *Financial Times*.

The back page of the *Financial Times* is a series of columns of company names. Each column is split into different headings. Looking more closely you will see that the headings, listed alphabetically, comprise about 40 different industries. Under each heading most of the major companies involved in that particular industry appear. Albright & Wilson appears under the Chemical heading:

| 1969 | | Stock | Closing Price | + % or − | Div. or Amt. | Times Cover-ed | Gross Yield % | P/E Ratio |
High	Low							
			CHEMICALS, PLASTICS, etc.					
18/3	10/0¾	Albr't Wilson	13/9xd	+/10½	15	1·1	5·5	16·5
11/9	7/-	Barrow B'rs'y	7/1½	+/1½	8½	1·2	4·8	17·4
57/-	32/-	Burt Boulton	42/6	◆	13	1·0	6·1	16·4

On the right hand side of the company's name there is a heading "closing price". Next to this is another figure, this time of +10½d. This indicates that yesterday's closing price was 10½d. more than the price the day before. In other words, the market in Albright & Wilson yesterday was firm and the price rose a little. The same was true of Barrow Barnsley which rose 1½d. On the left hand side of the company's name are two other figures under the heading of "1969 High Low." Look at these figures carefully. The price of Albrights has fluctuated between 18s. 3d. and 10s. 0¾d. in 1969. If you hold Albrights and do not have to raise cash you can watch those price movements with equanimity. They represent profits and losses which occur when the price rises or falls above or below what you paid for it. But these are only "paper" profits or losses. They only become real when you actually sell your shares. If you had brought Albright & Wilson at 10s. earlier in the year when the market was strong and needed the cash now, you could sell quite happily. But it would be a different matter if you had bought Burt Boulton earlier at 57s. and needed the money now, since the shares stand at only 42s. 6d. It would be of little consolation to reflect that Burt Boulton could easily be 100s. next year. Saving through shares is long-term saving!

Dividends, Earnings and Yields

The nominal or "par" value of the Albright & Wilson shares is 5s. and this is put in brackets against the company's name. Where no figure is shown against a company's name, that means the par value of the share is £1. Do not fall into the common mistake of so many investors: the only connection of the "par" value with the share price is a very indirect one through the dividend.

The last four columns are concerned with the cover and the safety of the income that you receive from your investment. The first column is the dividend per cent or amount. Sometimes companies declare their intention of paying a dividend of so many pence, i.e., 6d. a share. More often they express it as a percentage of the par value of the share. Albright has recently paid a 50 per cent dividend and those who buy the shares now buy it less the dividend. This is indicated by "xd"—or ex-dividend.

The question of "dividend" and "dividend yield" is something that confuses many investors. The "dividend," rather like the "coupon" on a government stock, is the amount of money paid out by the company to its shareholders. But this is not the same as the return on their money that investors expect to get, for they will be paying much more for their shares than their "par value."

If you could buy Albright & Wilson shares at 5s. then that "dividend" and the return on invested money, or "dividend yield," would be the same. But you cannot. Albright shares cost 13s. 9d. to buy. So the dividend yield is not 15 per cent but

$$\frac{\text{Nominal Value of the Share} \times \text{Dividend}}{\text{Price of Share.}}$$

In the case of Albright & Wilson this is

$$\frac{\text{5s.} \times \text{15 per cent}}{\text{13s. 9d.}} = \text{5·5 per cent.}$$

This is the figure which you will find in the second last
column of the F.T. table as "gross yield per cent." It is
"gross" because it is calculated before tax. The real return
on your money is even smaller than 5·5 per cent. It is 5·5
per cent × ·5875—this figure is the decimal for 11s. 9d.,
the amount of £1 left after tax at 8s. 3d.—which equals
3·23 per cent.

A further figure is called "Times Covered." Companies
do not pay out all of their profits to shareholders. Some of
it is retained in the business for further expansion. In
order to know how much the company could have paid out
and so be able to compare it with the actual dividend, investment analysts work out a figure called "Earnings."
This is the total profits of the company, after payment of all
prior charges, etc., available for the Ordinary shareholder.
This is calculated, in the same way as the dividend, as a
percentage of the nominal capital of the company. If the
earnings are divided by the dividend, the result is "Times
Covered" or the amount of times that the dividend could
have been paid if the directors had wished to distribute
everything. From the table it can be seen that Albright &
Wilson paid 15 per cent last year. The dividend is covered
1·1 times. 15 × 1·1 equals earnings of 16·5 per cent. The
same calculation can be done for Burt Boulton, but
the mark against that figure means something different.
The black diamond indicates that the company is in the
process of merging or re-organising its business.

But you will also come across something called an
"Earnings Yield." Earnings Yields bear the same re-
lation to earnings as Dividend Yields do to dividends.
They are calculated in the same way, i.e.,

$$\frac{\text{Nominal Value} \times \text{Earnings}}{\text{Price of Share}} \text{ so that}$$

Albright & Wilson earnings yield would be

$$\frac{5s. \times 16 \cdot 5}{13s.\ 9d.} = 6 \text{ per cent.}$$

Earnings and dividends can be compared. Earnings yields and dividend yields can also be compared. Earnings divided by dividends will give "Times Covered" as in the case of Albright: $16 \cdot 5$ per cent divided by 15 per cent = $1 \cdot 1$. Earnings yields divided by dividend yields give the same answer also: 6 per cent divided by $5 \cdot 5$ per cent = $1 \cdot 1$. And the dividend yield multiplied by "Times Covered" will produce the earnings yield: $5 \cdot 5$ per cent multiplied by $1 \cdot 1$ per cent = 6 per cent.

Why Earnings are Important

These figures can be worked out, as explained above, from the F.T. They can also be obtained from the *Moodie's* or *Exchange Telegraph* cards that your stockbroker will keep (*see* Chapter 5). The earnings figure is important for many reasons. It gives an idea of the safety of the dividend. For reasons connected with "gearing" (*see* Appendix A) or the amount of prior charges borrowing that a company has, such as Debentures and Preference shares, it is not true to say that if a company's dividend is twice covered by earnings, then even if profits fell by half it could still pay the same dividend. But beware of a dividend which is only once covered and steer well clear of the dividend which is "short earned" or not covered by earnings—any dividend covered by less than $1 \cdot 0$ times is short earned. Secondly, if the earnings figure is high, it suggests that the company could pay more in dividends if it wanted to. Thirdly, if earnings are increasing every year, then here again there is a good reason to assume that the dividend will also be raised. Fourthly, the earnings figure gives part of the answer as to how much money the company is spending on new equipment, research and expansion. If a manufacturing or trading company does not keep some of its profits for this purpose, it is going to find itself in trouble. Finally, the difference between what the company earns and what it pays out is going back into the company—and if it is at all competently run it should be increasing the asset value of your shares, i.e., the buildings, the equipment and the know-how which the shares represent. Other papers carry Stock Exchange prices but none give as much information as is given by the *Financial Times*.

Price Earnings Ratio

However, the earnings yield is much less important than it used to be. As a result of the introduction of Corporation Tax, most investment analysts prefer to talk of the price earnings ratio (PER or PE). This is because the PER expresses the market price of a share as a multiple of the earnings per share. This enables one share to be compared directly with another. The PER is calculated by dividing the share price by the earnings per share. So, if the share price is 20s. and the earnings per share, after Corporation Tax, are 2s. per share, then the price earnings ratio is $\frac{20s.}{2s.} \times 1$ or a PE ratio of 10:1, for the price represents 10 times the company's last annual earnings, or 10 years purchase of earnings. So, other things being equal, a share with a PER of 10 is cheaper than another with a PER of 12. Still, other things are not equal in share investment and it is not quite as simple as this. Some companies have easy markets in which to operate, others difficult ones. Some have young and aggressive management while others suffer from antiquated ways of doing things. Some have plenty of liquid assets with which to take advantage of opportunities while others are desperately short of money and need to borrow from their bank or their shareholders. All these considerations affect the price of a share and, therefore, the PER. Still, even if the PER is not the only guide to comparative value, it is still a worthwhile guide. A company must have exceptional prospects to be worth buying on a PER of 40 when other good companies are selling on PER's of 10.

In discussion with your broker you probably decide to buy some Albright & Wilson shares, and you leave him with an order to buy you 100.

The Jobber

The stockbroker is your agent. He is not allowed to buy and sell the shares for you on his own account, and so he must find someone from whom to buy the shares for you. This person is called the jobber and he deals only with stockbrokers. Jobbers specialise in certain shares and they buy for what they call their "book." As they generally do not wish to be "long" or "short" of a share—that is to buy more than they sell or vice versa—in case rapid fluctuations in prices cause them to make a capital loss, they are continually changing the prices they quote in order to keep their books straight. The jobber makes his living, not by commission as does the stockbroker, but from the difference at which he is prepared to buy and sell. This is called the jobber's "turn."

Your broker will approach the jobber specialising in Albright & Wilson and ask him without disclosing whether he is a buyer or seller "What are Albright & Wilson?" The answer may be 12s. 6d to 13s. 9d. That is, the jobber will buy them at 12s. 6d. and sell them at 13s. 9d. Your broker will then obtain quotations from other jobbers specialising in Albright & Wilson, and perhaps one of them will be a little long on Albright. He does not want to buy any more and would be only too happy to sell a few, and he therefore quotes a price of 12s. 3d. to 13s. 6d. Your broker will then tell him that he is a buyer of 100 and the deal, without anything further happening, has then been transacted.

A lot of people wonder why jobbers should get paid for standing around apparently doing nothing. In fact the jobber supplies a vital function and all stock exchanges, in Britain and abroad, have had to solve this in various ways. The jobber acts as a clearing house. Without him the stockbroker would spend half his time rushing around the City to find another stockbroker with a client who had 100 Albright & Wilson to sell. The jobber makes the market. By always being prepared to buy and sell the shares of even the smallest and least-known companies, he allows you and everyone else to trade in those shares if you want to. But for him, many shares would be completely unsaleable.

The Bill

As soon as your stockbroker has dealt in the Exchange, you are the owner of the shares and you owe him the money for them. The next morning you should receive his contract note. On this form will be specified the full title of the shares you bought and the price you paid per share. This may differ from the price you expected to pay. One reason is that you may have taken the middle price from the newspaper quotation rather than the actual buying price; the other is that since the newspaper obtained its quotations, prices might have moved. The amount the shares actually cost—13s. 6d. times 100 or £67 10s.—is called the consideration. This, however, is not the end of it, for buying shares is, unfortunately, rather expensive. First, on each buying transaction there is a government tax. This is the 1 per cent stamp duty on the consideration money. Then there is the 2s. 6d. transfer fee that most companies charge to register your name as a shareholder. These two sums are generally called together "stamp and fee." In this case it is 16s. Then there is the commission or fee for your stockbroker's services. This depends on the price of the shares and a minimum scale laid down by the Stock Exchange Council. It is about $1\frac{1}{4}$ per cent. On a share of 13s. 6d. it would be approximately 2d. per share or a further £16 8s. Finally there is a 2s. contract stamp so that the total amount you owe to your stockbroker is £69 2s. 8d. See that you check your contract note before you send your cheque off—even stockbrokers' clerks make mistakes.

Important Notice

Stamp duty, buying and selling commissions and the contract stamp and fee come to about 5 per cent. Then there is the jobber's turn—another 5 per cent. So you do not break even until your shares have gone up by 10 per cent in price.

Paying the Bill

The Stock Exchange has an odd way of settling its bills For trading purposes the year is split into 24 accounts 20 of a fortnight and 4 of three weeks. Every account begins on a Monday and ends on a Friday and payment for the shares bought during the Account is not due until settlement day—which is a Tuesday, 11 days after the end of the account. This delay is to allow time for all the paper work that is involved to be done by the Stock Exchange clerks. If you had bought your Albright & Wilson shares during the account running from Monday, November 24th to Friday, December 5th, 1969, you would see on the top of your contract note "bought for settlement December 16th, 1969." Make sure you pay your stockbroker before settlement day. He has got to settle his own bills then, and if you do not settle yours, you are causing him to lose money unnecessarily.

There are dozens of technicalities concerned with accounts and settlement days but most are for speculators and need not concern the investor. However, there is one worth knowing. If you sell shares and then use the proceeds from that sale to buy other shares, either during the same account or the one following, then the broker can charge only half commission on the smaller of the two deals. The Stock Exchange rules say, "at the broker's discretion," but this concession is given to virtually everyone who asks for it, so if you are not getting it ask the reason why.

Getting the Goods

Your 100 Albright & Wilson shares become yours as soon as the stockbroker came to terms with the jobbers. However, it may be some time before all the paper work is completed and it is registered in the books of Albright & Wilson. Some time after receiving the contract note you will receive the transfer form. This is the legal document transferring ownership of the shares. In recent years this document has been greatly simplified and now the only signature necessary is that of the "transferor" (i.e., the seller of the shares). It sets out in logical form the consideration money, i.e., the cost of the shares, the name of the company whose shares are being sold and details of the type of share, both in words and figures. Then follows the signature of the transferor, and the name and address of the person buying the shares. Finally, if you are the seller and not the buyer do not be upset if the consideration stated on the transfer form is more than the amount you yourself got for the shares. You are not being cheated by your stockbroker. It is just that the shares you sold have probably changed hands several times at several different prices between the moment you sold them and the moment the person who is sending the transfer form to you bought them. Finally, a long time after, because of the slowness of registration in this country, you will actually receive a share certificate. Keep it carefully—it represents money.

4

PROFESSIONAL MANAGEMENT FOR THE AMATEUR INVESTOR

If you want to invest successfully—and that means to increase both your income and capital—you are going to have to spend time and effort on deciding what and when to buy and sell. Many people are not able to do this but it does not mean that they have to give up hope of being able to protect their savings from inflation through Ordinary share investment. But what it does mean is that if they are not prepared to give the time themselves then they will have to find professional advisers to do it for them. Fortunately this is neither so expensive nor so difficult as you might imagine. In fact, it can be done simply and cheaply by buying the shares of Investment Trusts or the shares, sometimes called units, of Unit Trusts.

What are these Trusts?

Investment Trusts and Unit Trusts differ from each other in important ways but, despite this, they resemble each other more than they resemble anything else. An Investment or Unit Trust's business is to increase its profits and thus the income of its owners who are the shareholders in the case of a public company or Investment Trust, the Unit holders in the case of a Unit Trust. The profits of a trust do not come from making or selling things but from buying securities, which pay dividends. And the way it increases its profits is not by selling or making things better and more cheaply than its rivals but by the skill and care with which it chooses its securities. The first Investment Trust was formed nearly a century ago, the first

Unit Trust only in 1931, but the essence of both types of trust is the spreading of risk. There are risks in buying Ordinary shares which even the most far-sighted investor cannot always avoid, but these risks can be minimised by buying the shares of many different companies in lots of different industries. Few private investors, however are so rich that they can compete with trusts whose holdings consist of hundreds of shares in dozens of industries in several countries. Even if a considerable number of a trust's holdings do turn out to be disappointments, the others are more than sufficient protection to the trust's income and thus its dividend payment. Further, these trusts are all run by men whose whole lives are devoted to the correct assessment of securities and the benefits of this professional management constitute, with the spreading of the risk, the two main advantages of Investment or Unit Trust investment. Another important consideration is that only by buying the shares of these trusts can the ordinary saver hope to invest in foreign securities. The much faster growth of the national economies of western Europe make the shares of companies in these countries very attractive to the equity shareholder. But problems of distance, language, different legal requirements, price and foreign exchange make it almost impossible for the usual private investor to buy anything other than British shares with safety. The Investment and Unit Trusts, with their research staffs and international contacts, can do this easily, and nearly all Trusts have large holdings of foreign, particularly American, shares. Nowadays, when the British investor can only buy foreign securities by acquiring "premium dollars" the advantage of having professional management for foreign investment is even greater. The object of the fluctuating but more expensive "premium dollar" its to discourage British investors from investing abroad, and thus adding to the strain on the balance of payments. The premium on these funds for overseas investment can fluctuate very widely, and on the sale of a foreign security some of the premium dollars have to be surrendered to the Treasury as a form of tax. Thus the advantages of having a professional dealing with it are great.

Investment Trusts

An Investment Trust starts off with a sum of money, called its capital, just like any other company. This capital can be split into Debenture or Loan capital and Preference and Ordinary share capital. This has the important result of "gearing" Investment Trust companies (*see* Appendix A). Investment Trusts, also, are limited liability companies with boards of directors and shareholders and regulated by the Companies Act rather than by special Board of Trade directives. This freedom allows these trusts to retain part of their yearly income—generally between 20 and 25 per cent—and this in turn gives them very great freedom in deciding on their investment policies. The reserves that they are able to build up in this way give the investor protection against any recurrence of the terrible calamities of the 1930s. Although it is unlikely to happen again because of the greater power that governments now have over national economies, Investment Trust managers do not allow themselves to forget the Stock Exchange slump and the great depression of the 1930s. But a more important effect is to give the managers great freedom of manoeuvre in deciding when to raise new money. Of course, no one is lucky enough or clever enough always to raise money when it is cheap and to be able to buy shares when they are depressed, but the record of the companies in raising new money at favourable periods for new investments has been remarkably good. There are no statutory restrictions as to what Investment Trusts can invest in. Many of them consider it their duty to help British industry by putting part of their money behind small new companies and thus help build them up to a size where they can become public. Part of the Trust's money is also used to help the recovery of famous companies that have fallen on bad times. Of course, this is not done for nothing. The Trusts gain from this because they are able to buy the shares of these companies at very favourable prices. Although the trusts cannot distribute any capital gains they make in this way as dividends (if they did they would lose their special tax privileges and have to pay a tax on capital gains), these gains help to swell the company's reserves. The shareholder benefits ultimately because these reserves enable the Trust to increase its holdings of shares and thus improve both its profits and the dividend it pays.

There are disadvantages. Investment Trusts do not go in for advertising and are still hardly known outside the City. Further, their shares are like any other shares and the price is determined by supply and demand and not by the actual asset value of the share when it is bought or sold —that is, the value of all the trust's holdings of shares at their current market price divided by the number of the Investment Trust's shares. In fact, Investment Trust shares until recently have sold at substantially less than the asset value. Another difficulty is that the market in most Investment Trust shares is "narrow," that is, there are not many shares about. The reason for this is that Investment Trusts are popular with professional investors as well as with amateurs and although the supply of shares has been greatly increased by "rights" and "scrip" issues and by splitting shares of a high nominal value into several smaller ones, the fact remains that most people who buy Investment Trust shares buy for good. The result of a narrow market is that prices tend to move upwards and downwards more violently than the price of a share which is easily bought and sold. This means that Investment Trust shares are generally difficult to buy on a rising market and difficult to sell on a falling one.

The Unit Trust

Unit Trusts do not have capital in any real sense. Indeed, they are not companies but really co-operative ventures. A trustee company, nearly always a bank or insurance company and responsible for the safe-keeping of the share certificates of the trust, and a management company, control of which must be entirely separate from that of the trustee company, together set up a trust. This trust buys a selection of shares. The trust then sells units to the public. The price of these units, both for buying and selling, is calculated according to a Board of Trade formula and depends on the actual market value of the shares held by the trust. These prices are calculated daily and the managers are always prepared to buy or sell units at these prices. There is a slight difference in the buying and selling price to allow the management company to cover its dealing costs. The amount of profits that the management company can make is also strictly regulated by the Board of Trade. All Unit Trusts have a fixed life, more often than not of 21 years, and an upper limit to the number of units that can be sold. Generally speaking, when a Unit Trust nears the end of its life, the unit holders can either vote to prolong its life or it can be wound up and the assets distributed to the holders.

Originally Unit Trusts had a fixed list of shares which they could buy, but this turned out to be most unsatisfactory and all are now "flexible" or "managed" trusts which can buy nearly all shares traded on the Stock Exchange. However, many still specialise in particular sections of the market and there are Unit Trusts specialising in Investment Trust companies, insurance companies, bank companies, atomic and electronic industries, etc.

Unit Trusts are at a disadvantage compared with Investment Trusts. First, they have no gearing, although this is becoming rapidly less important. Most Investment Trusts, faced with a choice of raising new money at about 4% by a rights issue of Ordinary shares, or at 6 or 7% by the issue of a prior charge, choose the cheaper method. And this means that their own gearing is getting lower and lower. Secondly, Unit Trusts are required by their Trust Deeds to distribute all their income to shareholders. Thus, they are unable to build up reserves against a rainy day, although it must be admitted that no Unit Trust has ever failed to make a distribution. But it also means that the managers are not able to take such a long investment view as those of an Investment Trust, for they must buy and sell equities as the money comes in and goes out. If there are net sales to the public, that is, more units are sold by the managers to the public than are bought back from former holders, then the Trust is getting new money to invest. If the opposite happens and there are net purchases by the managers, then the Trusts have to sell securities in order to pay for the units that they have bought back. Finally, although the choice of investments before Unit Trusts is now much wider, they are still unable to invest as adventurously as the Investment Trust. Nevertheless, the record of the well-managed Unit Trusts, despite these disadvantages, has compared favourably with the market as a whole, particularly as shown by the *Financial Times* index. The odds are that if you have invested since 1960, you would have done far better for yourself by buying Unit Trusts than by buying your own shares direct.

The Choice
There is little doubt that you will do better in a well-managed Investment Trust than in a Unit Trust, however

good; a poorly managed Trust of any description is no use to anyone. But Unit Trusts do have their advantages. You can buy Investment Trusts only through a stockbroker. Unit Trusts can be bought through a broker, but you can also buy direct from the managers, through a bank, solicitor or accountant, or by replying to newspaper advertisements. There are two types of advertisements. One merely tells you about the advantages and characteristics of a particular Unit Trust and invites you to buy at the price prevailing for the units on the day that the managers receive your letter. The other is an advertisement by which a specific number of shares at a given price are offered to the public. One Trust, called Scotbits, is sold "over the counter" of the Scottish Joint Stock banks. Dealings in Scotbits increased substantially when this method of buying was introduced. Prices asked are those quoted in the previous day's *Financial Times*. However, it is again an expensive method of selling and the English banks have not been prepared to take it up. However, the National Westminster Group of Banks sell the "Westminster Hambro Unisavings Bond" over the counter and most of the major banks have their own Unit Trusts which, while not sold directly over the counter, can conveniently be bought by any customer who asks.

The Amounts Involved

If you want to buy an Investment Trust, not only will you need a stockbroker, but you will need at least £100. You need only £25 or so of savings to buy Unit Trusts. But a lot of people do not even have this—about a third of the population in fact—and so virtually all of the trusts have produced savings schemes. The idea of this is that you run an account with the managers of the Trust and send them subscriptions either regularly or whenever you can afford it. As soon as your account has enough cash to buy one unit, that is bought for you and any cash left over is kept to be added to your further subscriptions. Anyone can afford this for the smallest subscription is 5s. a month.

Apart from being a safe and painless way of buying Ordinary shares and thus protecting your savings, savings plans are also a cheap method. This is because of what is called "pound cost averaging." Say that you are saving 10s. a week or £2 a month. In the first month the buying price of the unit is 7s. 6d. For your £2 you are able to buy 5 units with 2s. 6d. carried forward to the next month. Next month the units are 10s. Therefore your savings of £2 plus the 2s. 6d. from the previous month only enable you to buy 4 units. Once again 2s. 6d. is carried over to the next month. In the third month the market may suffer a setback and the units drop to 6s. With £2 2s. 6d. again, this means that you can buy 7 units with 6d. to carry forward to the following month. The average cost of the units over the 3 months has been:

	Cost per unit*	
	s.	d.
First Month	7	6
Second Month	10	0
Third Month	6	0
	23	6
Average cost per unit per month	7	10.

The actual price you have paid for your units, though, has been:

		£	s.	d.
First Month	5 Units for	1	17	6
Second Month	4 Units for	2	0	0
Third Month	7 Units for	2	2	0
	16 Units	5	19	6
Average per unit			7	3½.

* In fact, no unit trust would fluctuate as wildly in price as this.

This saving may not seem very much but over a period of years, and with the sort of fluctuations that you must expect, it does represent a considerable saving (here 6½d. on 7s. 10d.)

Lastly, units can always be easily sold or bought at a fixed figure, and their price represents the actual value of the trust's holdings. Market rumour and confidence have nothing to do with a Unit Trust price as they do with that of an Investment Trust. A further factor is that the administration of a Unit Trust is supervised by the trustee, and as these are generally the biggest banks or insurance companies, this means something. The Board of Trade also keeps a supervisory eye on them. And to those that are interested in what the Unit Trusts hold, their holdings of shares are published twice yearly so that it is still possible for the investor, if he wishes to do so, to follow not only the price movements of his unit, but also those of the actual companies of which he is a shareholder through his Unit Trust. All these factors add up to a safe and simple means of investment.

Which Trust to Buy

It is no use buying just any Trust. It is absolutely vital to buy one with a good record of management. This is an extremely difficult quality to assess, but it can be, and is, done. If you are buying Investment Trusts your stockbroker ought to know the comparative records of the biggest and best-known Investment Trusts, the discount on their asset value at which they can be bought, and the market's view of the quality of management. Assessing Unit Trusts is a little easier since questions of how much of the yearly profits are retained and the time of raising new money are not complicating factors in looking at the management record. A Unit Trust which has not beaten the *Financial Times* Index—that means doing better in

good times and not falling so much in bad times—is worse
than useless.

Equity Linked Life Assurance

Earlier it was said that no one should begin to invest on
the Stock Exchange until they had begun to buy their own
house and certainly not until they had life assurance.
However, it is now possible for you to have this cake and
eat it too because of the development of a new form of life
assurance which has become known as an "equity linked
life assurance endowment policy." This type of policy first
appeared in the early 1960s but did not become a major
factor until after 1965. Since then the sale of this type of
life assurance has grown enormously and now accounts for
more than twenty-five per cent of all new life assurance
premiums written.

With an ordinary life assurance policy, the premiums
that you pay to the life assurance company are invested by
them in a variety of things—government stocks, company
debentures and other fixed interest securities, property,
and shares quoted on the Stock Exchange. This "portfolio"
is valued—sometimes every year, but more generally every
three years—by the actuaries of the life assurance company
who decide how much profit—both realised and unrealised—has been made by the company on its investments and then, on the basis of these profits, the company
declares "bonuses" to its policy holders. These bonuses
are extra to the amount of money that the company has
promised to pay on your life endowment policy, either at
the end of the plan—or maturity of the endowment policy—
or at your death if this occurs earlier. Such policies are
known as endowment policies "with profits" and can mean
that the actual amount paid out at maturity is more than
twice as much as the basic figure promised.

The success or otherwise of investment departments of

various assurance companies can be seen from the different levels of bonuses that companies are able to declare. Although the individual policy holder benefits from the success of his assurance company's investment policy, he does not know how well or how badly the company is doing *now* because the bonuses declared refer back to profits made in earlier years. In addition, the companies are traditionally very cautious in estimating their investment profits, particularly valuations of unrealised capital gains, and in the past some policy holders have felt that not enough of the profits made on their premiums were coming through to them as bonuses but instead were being kept in the company as "reserves" for the future.

So some life assurance companies began to offer a much more direct investment to would-be policy holders; they promised to invest premiums directly into a unit trust. This way the policy holder could tell from day to day how well his investment was doing by looking at the price of the unit trust in his newspaper. Moreover, instead of his premiums disappearing into the enormous unpublished investment portfolio of the average assurance company, the policy holder could get a vicarious thrill from following the fortunes of the individual shares held by the unit trust. Depending on the type of policy the dividends on the units are used to buy new units for the policy holder or kept by the company which uses them to declare "bonuses" to existing policy holders instead.

In addition, these new companies publicised the fact that anyone buying life assurance was entitled to tax relief on the premiums, which can be as much as 16% of the yearly premium. Naturally the "life cover" of that policy does cost a certain amount of money and there is also a management charge to the unit trust but, taken together, these costs do not amount to anything near 16%, so that savers buying a unit trust through a life assurance endowment policy are, in effect, buying their units at a substantial discount on the market price. Finally, buying in this regular manner brings with it all the advantages of pound cost averaging, simplifies the whole problem of share selection, and avoids the need for a "lump sum" with which to begin buying shares.

Although these equity linked policies began originally as a simple method of allowing savers to invest in stock market securities at a discount, the life assurance side became steadily more important. One of the problems of such a policy is that because the premiums are invested in units of a unit trust, the value of the policy at death or on maturity very much depends on the level of the stock market. If the Stock Exchange is doing well, then cash values will be high; but if it is doing badly the encashment value of the policy could well be less than the total amount of the premiums that have been paid. To counteract this assurance companies produced guaranteed minimum values either on the death of the policy holder or on the maturity of the policy. This means that the policy holder has a choice—a minimum cash sum or the units allocated to the policy. If money is needed on maturity, then you can take the cash but if you have no need for cash immediately, then you can take the units and sell them for cash at your own convenience. In addition, it is now possible to borrow against the surrender of some of these equity linked policies, just as it has always been possible for the policy holder to borrow against the value of an ordinary endowment policy.

As a result of the success of these policies, there are now several other types of equity linked assurance. The most important are equity linked annuities, "whole life" policies and insurance "bonds." These bonds are designed to enable investors to have the tax advantages of insurance with a "lump sum" investment in shares or property. In addition, the building societies have introduced a similar type of endowment assurance scheme but linked to investment in deposits of building societies. These policies are designed for those who want to save regularly for house purchase, since the building society gives policy holders the same preferential treatment for house loans as they do to their direct depositors. Most of the policies have low surrender penalties, so that although the policy, as such, is no use for buying a house, it can be converted into cash easily and cheaply. However, the only growth in these plans comes through the compounding of interest; there is no "growth" in the sense of capital appreciation as with stock exchange equities or properties.

Nearly all the major assurance companies now sell their own equity linked endowment policies which are invested either in an independent unit trust or in their own specially formed trust. There are now several dozen such policies on the market and, since an equity endowment policy ought to be taken out for at least fifteen years, the problem of choice is difficult. There are two questions that you must ask yourself before joining any of these policies. The first is does the policy suit you? You can get advice on this from magazines such as *Planned Savings* and the *Unitholder*, and a good person to consult is an insurance broker, although there is one proviso to this—the commission rates on many equity policies are lower than those on conventional policies and this sometimes creates a bias on the broker's part in favour of the latter. An important consideration with any policy is its surrender value—how much will you get if you do not wish to continue with the plan? Some policies are known as "front end loaded" with most of the commissions and other costs of setting up the policy taken out of the first year's premium; this could be more than 50% and, of course, this is all money lost as far as you are concerned if you decide to surrender the policy after three or four years. Other companies take a percentage every year but charge high surrender penalties if you stop the policy. Another important factor is that if you want to borrow against the policy or use it for house purchase, it must have a guaranteed maturity and death value. Finally, at maturity you should have the choice of taking either cash or units and obviously this will depend on your own personal situation and preference at that time.

The second major question is how good are the investment advisers managing the unit trust and, if they are good, will they remain so? A slightly better capital performance of one trust over another can more than compensate for higher insurance costs. The important point to remember is that this type of policy is long term and, if the scheme is at all successful, the investment fund—or unit trust—will become a very substantial one indeed, investing many millions of pounds a year. Picking the league leaders of the unit trust movement on a year-to-year basis is not a very satisfactory way of choosing your policy because small funds can perform extremely well while they are small but do not always continue to give so sparkling a performance once they have grown to a reasonable size of £5 million or so. Secondly, many of the really successful funds are new funds, often being promoted by a new management company. By the very nature of things, not only does the unit trust grow bigger but the investment managers also change, and what is today a bright, young and aggressive management team may well have broken up tomorrow and gone to half a dozen different competitive management companies. So, whilst you must look for investment performance, you must also look at the size of the management company and the likelihood of it still being in existence ten years from today. Obviously, the major banks and insurance companies and the two or three major unit

trust groups of comparable size and standing, and similar
need to maintain their corporate image, have no choice but
to continue to produce reasonably good investment results
whatever difficulties they may have with individual
managers who leave their employ. And these companies
all have experience of running investment funds handling
not millions but hundreds of millions of pounds.

But is an equity linked policy better than a conventional
with-profits policy? This cannot be answered with a simple
yes or no and strong views are held by the advocates of
different types. There is no doubt that the assurance
companies can be much more flexible in their investment
policies than the unit trusts. Indeed, because of taxation
considerations, a trust manager can only really invest in
equity shares. An assurance company manager can invest
in almost everything, depending on the state of the stock
market and the economic situation, a fact which gives him
considerable freedom in switching his funds from fixed
interest stocks to equities, from property to shares.
This is one of the keys to investment success, for although
the long-term trend of the stock market is upwards, there
are long periods when the trend is downwards or sideways.

Assurance companies have another advantage. As a
policy holder of an equity linked scheme, your returns
depend to a great extent upon the level of the stock market
at the time your policy matures. There can be no certainty
as to the actual amount you will receive for your policy
above the guaranteed minimum. The assurance company
actuary in his triennial revaluations smoothes out the
fluctuations in the stock market and is able to promise his
policy holder a much more definite result; against this, of
course, he has to be cautious in valuing his capital gains so
that when the stock market is booming the conventional
policy holder does not do as well as the man in the pure
equity fund of the unit trust. The reason is that the actuary

is putting many of his profits into reserve, rather than passing them on to the policy holder immediately, so that when times are bad on the stock market, he is prepared and can use these reserves and still continue to declare good bonuses.

The major insurance companies still give the impression that they have entered into the equity linked endowment field, not because they believe in it, but because such policies are doing well at the moment and they feel that they must have such a policy in their armoury—even if they do not intend to push their sales too hard. In fact they are trying to make their conventional policies more attractive by improving their bonus rates and introducing other special types of bonuses. There is little doubt that if the companies really wanted to make straight equity linked policies work, they would set up special unit trust type funds within their investment portfolios and so gain the investment freedom that an assurance company has together with the sales advantage of a unit trust linked policy. Such a policy has yet to appear but this is probably only a matter of time. For the moment, you must make a choice between two policies, neither of which are perfect, and the choice in the end must depend solely on what policy best fits your own particular circumstances.

Other Professional Management

There are two other ways by which the investor who does not want to be bothered can safely invest directly. Both industries are composed of large units with specialised techniques, so that little competition from new entrants is to be feared, and both have above-average rates of growth. As both supply services which become more attractive as people become richer, this above-average growth can be expected to continue. One is insurance, the other is banking.

Insurance

Insurance is divided into two rather different industries—
life assurance and general insurance. Life business is long-
term and definite. The company has to pay out to the
customer one day, and so the companies have got to earn
a minimum rate of return on their premiums. Competition
and the need to bring down premiums ensure that the
companies try to earn more than the minimum necessary.
As a result, a growing proportion of life company funds
since the war have gone into equity shares or property.
The attraction of this to the investor is that the difference
between what the companies must earn and what they do
earn is "profit"—and much of this is attributable to the
shareholder. There is only one major proviso to this.
Many of the companies, to attract business from the non-
profit-making "mutual" offices and to offer a hedge
against inflation, have "with-profits" policies. This
means that some of the company's profits go to the
policy holders rather than to the shareholders but, even so,
there is enough to satisfy everyone in a well-managed
concern.

The composite companies are different, for besides life
business they have fire, marine and general accident
business. This type of business is a "once and for all"
matter. If your house does not burn down during the
course of the year, the company keeps the premium and
pays you nothing. If it does burn down, and many others
likewise, it has to pay out but it can increase insurance
premiums the following year. Many of the companies
have much of their business abroad so that, apart from
having to keep much of their money in easily realised form,
like short-dated Government stocks, they must keep some
of it in the bonds of foreign governments. Even so, they
can put some of this money into Ordinary shares. Since
they do not have to earn a fixed rate of interest on their

money, what they do earn is, so to speak, "profit" for the shareholder. As a result of their clever investment policy, the investment income of composite companies has now grown to be much larger than their underwriting profits.

Composite companies are attractive because their investment income gives the investor the safety and stability of an investment trust. But there are also the excellent growth prospects to come from a well run insurance business. The underwriting profits are important to the investor: investment income grows as the result of the good management of the money already invested but it also increases as more of an increasing premium income and good underwriting profits become available for investment in equities. But an underwriting loss, which can happen even to the best-managed company, does not mean that the company has to cut its dividend.

Commercial Banking

The case for banking shares is fairly obvious. Only 30 per cent of households in this country have banking accounts, compared with 80 per cent in America. This is one of the services that become more and more important as nations and individuals get richer. Further, the steady increase in business activity also means greater demands every year on the banking service. Naturally the profits of banks will be affected by government action, particularly credit squeezes. Nevertheless, bank earnings have grown at an above-average rate over the past decade, despite its unfortunate history of credit squeezes, and they will continue to grow well in the future.

The Choice

The quality of management will count just as much in these industries as it will anywhere else. But your broker should be able to tell you which companies have had the best record in the past and which look attractive for the future.

The Do-it-yourself Unit Trust

Despite their many advantages, not everyone is happy investing through investment or unit trusts. Investing through the medium of a management company takes the thrill out of backing one's own judgment against that of the market and, although it minimises likely losses, investing in this indirect way also minimises the gains that can be expected from a successful investment policy. On the other hand the individual who is going to invest directly will need both a considerable amount of money and a willingness to work fairly hard at it if he is to be successful. What is the answer for the saver who is prepared to spend time on his investments but, so far, has very little, or no capital at all, to invest? This was a problem that exercised most financial journalists during the great bull market of 1957-9 but, in the end, the answer adopted turned out to be an American one. This was the Investment Club or "Do-it-yourself" unit trust.

What is an Investment Club?

Investment clubs consist of a small group of friends or business acquaintances who jointly agree to pool part of their normal monthly savings to buy shares on the stock exchange. These groups are of all types—friends, husband and wife groups, office staff or research groups, school teachers or factory workers, church groups or labourers. The club generally meets once a month, either at the home of one of the members or in a place conveniently near where most of the members work, and agrees on a particular share to buy. The amount of money that each member contributes can vary tremendously—from 10s. a month upwards—but the average appears to be about £3. The size of the club also varies. The most important consideration is the monthly income of the club. Sums of as little as £30 or £40 can be invested in shares, but this is uneconomical to the investor and very unprofitable for the stockbroker. A monthly amount of at least £80 and preferably £100 is probably the minimum to go for, as such an investment will at least allow your stockbroker to cover his direct clerical expenses. On the other hand the clubs, as well as being sociable, are also meant to be educative. If the club is too big the more timid member will be inhibited from speaking and taking an active part in the club's affairs and thus the educative aspect of the club will be nullified. It seems that the ideal attendance number is about 15, but the number of subscribing members can easily be 30 or 40. In fact, there are clubs with many more members; the Pilot's Investment Club at London Airport has over 400 members.

Origins of the Investment Clubs

The first investment clubs were formed in America. The movement became popular in 1951 and has grown rapidly since then. There are now well over 30,000 clubs, of which about 6,500 are affiliated to the National Association of Investment Clubs of America, and they are believed to control investments of more than $400 million and to invest more than $6 million every month. As a result, they are now one of the more important investing institutions on the American stock exchanges. The first clubs began to be formed in England in 1958. Since then they have grown even faster, proportionately, than they did in America. By early 1960s there were approximately 1,750 clubs in existence; between them 35,000-40,000 savers were investing almost £2 million a year.

However, the introduction of short- and long-term capital

gains tax, which hit the administration of the clubs particularly hard, together with the difficult stock market conditions of the middle 1960s stopped the growth of investment clubs in Britain. Many clubs which were formed in the early halcyon days went out of existence but a considerable number struggled on despite the problems, and with many of the taxation difficulties eased by the Association of Investment Clubs, investors are beginning to form clubs again.

How to Start a Club

The best way of investing through a club is to start your own. This is not always possible, though, and for those unable or unwilling to do this the NAIC has a service which will put would-be members in touch with clubs in their own areas. Assuming that you can find sufficient friends interested in forming a club—and this always turns out to be much easier than you expect—the first thing to do is to write to the National Association of Investment Clubs Ltd., 17 Harrington Street, Liverpool L2 90A. You will then be sent information, in particular notes on forming an investment club, a suggested constitution and agenda for the first meeting, and some other general information.

5

HOW TO BE IN THE KNOW

Investment is an art and needs time devoted to it. Most people, however, regard the Stock Exchange as some great gambling casino where making money depends simply on luck and being on the "inside track" for good information. Thus, in private life their characteristics may be prudence, intelligence and courage, but as average investors on the stock exchange they become greedy, fearful and stupid. Their greed persuades them to buy shares on the most implausable take-over stories, their fearfulness together with their ignorance of the workings of the market makes them sell any good share that their broker can make them buy well before the true capital appreciation is obtained, while their ignorance allows them to attribute losses to the machinations of financial speculators rather than their own stupidity. Neither on the Stock Exchange nor anywhere else will you get "owt for nowt," and if you are not prepared to put up some time and effort as well as money for your investment the best advice is "don't invest." You will only lose money, either as an individual or a club.

What Makes Prices Move?

There is only a limited supply of shares of any particular company and the price of the share moves in accordance with supply and demand for it. The fundamental reason why its price moves up over a period of time is because more and more people want to buy it. They will want to buy it because it promises them an increasing income. Sometimes people begin to buy shares not because of the income they hope to get from them but simply because they expect to sell them quickly at a higher price to someone else a little later on. This speculative madness happens only rarely and never lasts for very long. The last time this sort of behaviour became really widespread was in 1929 in America. It ended in the Wall Street crash and, almost without exception, everybody involved, whether amateur or professional, lost everything. It could happen again.

Because equity shares and real estate offer the prospect of an increasing income, they are, when properly chosen, the best form of long-term saving. But because equity prices are determined by supply and demand, their short-term movements depend upon the confidence of the stock market as a whole. The factors that influence this are general ones referring to the political, economic and industrial outlook, and particular ones that have reference only to individual companies. You must know about these factors.

Political Events

These are the most difficult to assess and foretell, and it is therefore fortunate that they are not so important as is usually believed. It is always considered that the outcome of elections is tremendously important for the stock market and yet, contrary to expectations, prices stopped rising after the Conservative victory in 1959 and rose very rapidly after the Labour victories of 1964 and 1966. In the earlier case, any increase in the stock market's confidence as the result of a Conservative victory was more than outweighed by a depressing economic outlook. And although the economic outlook after the Labour victory was equally depressing, the stock market expected both inflation and possibly devaluation, and decided that equities were better than fixed interest savings. Of course, the possibility of a future Government pledged to increase taxation or change the nature of the ownership of various industries is a worrying factor to the stock market, but, in general, political bogies of this nature tend to be specialised, aiming at particular industries such as steel or property development, and short-lived. Once the deed is done, it is over and finished with and the stock market simply forgets it.

International political factors are much more important and fears of the expropriation of the assets of foreign-based companies, or a bloody revolution and complete economic breakdown, tend to keep the price of shares which are endangered by such possibilities fairly cheap. But they have little effect on the rest of the market. An international crisis depresses prices, but here again the long-term saver is not affected. As soon as the crisis is solved prices recover, and if it is not solved there will be plenty of other more important things to worry about.

The Economic Scene

This is the key to market confidence. The pound sterling, together with gold and the dollar, is used as an international currency. Its success in this role depends on the confidence of foreigners in the pound's strength remaining unimpaired. The only way in which foreigners are convinced that the pound is strong is by seeing that Britain's gold reserve, which backs it, is plentiful. Unfortunately, for reasons much too complicated to go into here, these gold reserves have never been more than just sufficient to keep foreigners happy. What has happened since the war is that a combination of governmental incompetence and business complacency has resulted in our exports, which would have helped to swell our gold reserves, increasing much more slowly than our imports. The effect has been that whenever the British economy has begun to expand as fast as other countries, as happened in 1955 and 1959, our gold reserves have begun to shrink and sooner or later the government, to stop a sterling crisis, has had to restrain the economy. This "stop-go-stop" economic policy has had a disastrous effect not only on the British economy, but also on many sections of British industry.

Not all companies are equally affected by governmental restrictive policies, and some even continue to increase their profits. But if economic growth is restrained all companies find it harder to make profits. More important, investors lose confidence in the ability of the companies in which they are shareholders to increase their profits and dividends. Indeed, as the squeeze tightens, more and more companies report lower, rather than higher, profits and some even cut their dividends. Share prices fall and, as no one wants to buy, they continue to drift slowly downwards. This serves to increase the market's pessimism. The share prices of companies which manage to increase their profits despite tougher trading conditions are affected by the general unhappiness and they do not rise as much as might have been expected in better times.

The Facts to Look For

What this means is that you must keep a fairly close eye on what is happening. The most important published statistics are probably those concerned with our trade balance. For various statistical reasons these monthly figures nearly always show a "trade-gap," i.e., we seem to be buying more from foreigners than we are selling to them. The actual monthly seasonally adjusted trade figures will continue to show, because of the way they are calculated, this "trade gap" and the investor needs to use a rule of thumb to estimate how well Britain is doing. If the monthly gap is about £30-40 million, then the overall balance of payments position is approximately in balance. If the monthly gap is less, then the balance of payments is in surplus and there is no need to fear for the strength of the pound sterling.

But if the gap is greater than £40 million, then the balance of payments is in overall deficit—and sooner or later the government will have to do something about it. That always means a nasty shock for the Stock Exchange. Another monthly figure is the size of our holding of gold and convertible currencies. For various reasons this is not as good a guide to the trade balance as it used to be but, read in conjunction with it, it gives a good indication of the strength of sterling. Beware if this begins to fall rapidly. The third statistic to watch is the dollar-pound exchange rate. At present this is allowed to fluctuate between $2·38-$2·42 to the £, and $2·40 is often referred to as "parity." If the exchange rate falls below the $2·40 and stays there, that is another danger signal. It shows that bankers and traders are losing confidence in the pound's strength.

The other important indicators to watch are those relating to the internal state of the economy. Post-war British governments have been obsessed, above all else, by the problem of inflation. It has come to be accepted as a rule of thumb that when the chart of the monthly figures of the unemployed crosses that of unfilled vacancies, showing that there are more jobs than men, the economy is "overheated" and inflation can be expected. Restrictions are usually imposed soon after. Other points to watch are the size of the various annual wage awards and movement in the retail price index; governments get quite excited if these show signs of increasing at above-average rates. The index of industrial production is an important indicator as to whether the overall level of economic activity is rising or falling, even though it is usually a couple of months out of date. Generally speaking, if the index is rising most firms should be finding a buoyant market for their goods, productivity of workers and machines should be increasing and profit margins ought to be improving. If the index is stationary or falling the opposite is usually true and there is no point in expecting an increase in industrial profits that year. The quarterly figures produced by the Board of Trade showing the trends of industrial profits, as well as the monthly figures produced by the *Financial Times*, are useful if used in conjunction with the index. Only if the index and industrial profits are rising, or look as though they soon will be rising, are higher share prices justified.

The Industrial Outlook

The national economy is growing in size every year, even though in some years growth is not as fast as it could be because of governmental action. Nevertheless, within this growing economy some industries are dying and others are being born, some cannot meet the demand on them and others are facing the problems of excess capacity. So you must look not only at the general state of the economy, but also at particular sections of it. The law of supply and demand still operates to determine profits, and this law has been strengthened by the Restrictive Trade Practices Court and the Monopolies Commission; the Common Market and increasing international competition will strengthen it still further.

Formerly, industries with surplus capacity could get together and fix prices. This is no longer possible, and so the cable makers and consumer durable manufacturers, to take two examples, must now fight it out with lower prices until the weaker companies and the excess capacity is eliminated. Other industries, such as steel and paper, have such large units of production that whenever they expand they cannot fail to face short periods of over-production. Companies in such industries at such times are unattractive to the investor. Other industries, cotton textiles and shipbuilding, for example, are no longer competitive even in the U.K. market and face only extinction or survival through Government subsidy. These are even less attractive to the investor. Still others, such as motor cars, for instance, depend to some extent for their prosperity upon a high level of tariff protection. The movement towards freer international trade makes such industries vulnerable to foreign competition and unattractive for investment until it is clear which companies will survive.

Where to Find the Facts

The amount of knowledge you need sounds fearsome, but fortunately nearly all of it comes predigested. If you are not interested in the Stock Exchange or in the economy, then the *Financial Times* looks very forbidding, but it is an indispensable aid to investing. It is remarkably well written, excellently informed and easy to read. More important, its articles on the economy and on various industries and particular companies are slanted for the needs of the investor and the information they contain often cannot be found anywhere else. Other daily and Sunday papers have City sections, though none can be anywhere near as informative as the *Financial Times*. Both *The Times* and the *Daily Mail* have excellent City pages, and both of them, in common with the *Financial Times*, have an index of share price movements which they publish daily. These indices are particularly useful as they demonstrate the market's feeling and show in one figure whether it is bullish, i.e., confident, or bearish, i.e., pessimistic. There is not only an index for the market as a whole, but a separate index for each section of the market. The indices run by these papers are all slightly different and some statisticians get quite heated as to which is best. For your own purpose those of the *Daily Mail* and *The Times* are probably better indicators of the market's movements than that of the

Financial Times, since both are much larger and newer, but it is the *Financial Times* which is read and considered important by the City. The *Daily Telegraph*, *Guardian*, *Scotsman* and the Sunday papers all have informative City sections, too. Then there are the weekly magazines. The *Economist* is mainly concerned with political, economic and industrial matters while the *Investor's Chronicle* is primarily concerned with companies and consists, apart from a few general articles on investing, of analyses of the companies which have reported the previous week. The information contained in these analyses is important to you in two ways. First, a company's actual trading experience and the chairman's comments can be used to estimate how well other companies in the same industry are doing. Secondly, these analyses will suggest to you companies which it will be worth your while to investigate further and perhaps buy.

Company Records and Card Services

Professional investors keep the accounts of all companies in which they are interested as well as any cuttings which have appeared in the financial papers. Even so, they need some way of seeing at a glance all the relevant information about a company. To do this they need the statistical record services provided by *Moodie's Services* or the *Exchange Telegraph Company*. These cards are absolutely vital to those who have no knowledge of a company. They are the only means of obtaining all the information available on a company, and particularly its financial record. These services cost a great deal of money and are well beyond the means of the ordinary investor. However, this is not true in the case of your broker; he should be able to obtain for you any card that you need.

Description and Record

The information supplied by these two services is similar, although the lay-out is slightly different. *Moodie* uses a second, smaller card for news about companies that appears between balance sheet dates, whilst the *Exchange Telegraph* puts everything on to the same card. The cards are headed by the name of the company, its previous name if any, its business and a paragraph listing subsidiaries and the products that they make. Underneath this comes a list of the directors. Next comes the company's capital structure, on the left-hand side the different types and amounts of capital that its shareholders have authorised it to issue, and on the right the actual amounts that have been issued. Underneath this is a brief history of the companys' capitalisation, showing any reorganisations, rights or scrip issues. Underneath this again there is quite often a heading giving dates when the dividend is due on either or both the Preference and Ordinary shares, and if, and under what circumstances, the Preference are redeemable, and information about voting rights.

The main body of the sheet is then taken up by the financial record of the company for the last ten years or so. What is put in and how it is laid out depends a great deal on what the company itself gives in its own accounts but, in general, the information given is fairly standard. The first column shows the amount of *Ordinary Capital* issued. Next comes the *amount brought in*, an accounting figure which is unimportant to you. Then there is the company *trading profit*, roughly the difference between the price at which it produced its goods or services and the price it got for them. This is one of the most important figures. After this comes all the company's expenses. The first and most important is *depreciation*. The company's factories and machines all wear out after a while. If, when it is using them, it does not put aside money for their renewal, the company is living off its capital and, sooner or later, will be left with nothing. This is therefore an important figure to watch. The column showing *directors' remuneration* and other expenses are not particularly important. This usually includes the accountants' fees for auditing the company's books. Then the government takes its share and this will either appear as a single *taxation* column, or be split between *income tax*, 8s. 3d. in the pound, and *profits tax*, which is another 3s. However, since the introduction of Corporation Tax in 1965, the cards show only one column tax —Corporation Tax which is now at 45% though it originally started at 40%. The next column shows the *net profits* after tax and all expenses; the following one shows the *amount taken for paying the Preference dividends*. After that comes the *net profits after Preference dividends* have been paid. This last figure is sometimes known as the "earned for Ordinary" because this is all owned by the Ordinary shareholders. It is an extremely important figure. Because companies usually declare their dividends before tax and as a percentage of the nominal value of the capital, the "earned for Ordinary" is expressed in the same way, i.e., as a percentage, and is then known as the *earnings* figure. After the *earnings* and *dividend* figures come other figures. These are always headed *Appropriations*. This is because the directors have no choice about paying depreciation, tax, and Preference dividends but can decide to deal with the remaining profits as they wish. In practice, they always pay out some in dividends and the remainder they appropriate to various funds, the most common being "general reserves." In other words, this money, together with the depreciation, is ploughed back into the business. This money is often referred to as "cash flow," meaning the amount of money the company has coming in for modernisation and expansion. Obviously a company with a large cash flow in relation to its capital commitments is much less likely to have to ask its shareholders to subscribe more money by a "rights" issue. Underneath all this are various notes referring to particular figures in the columns.

Priority Percentages

The next heading is Priority Percentages and is most important to the equity investor for this shows how safe the equity dividend is. The first one or two figures show the amount of money needed to pay Preference share-holders and other prior charges, both as absolute totals and also as a percentage of the net earnings. The last figures show the amount needed for the equity dividend and its percentage of total earnings and the share of the profits appropriated for other purposes. These are the important ones. If the percentage of the earnings needed to pay the equity dividend is high, between 70 and 80%, say, it is fairly obvious that if profits fall at all badly the divid-end is going to be cut. This is never popular with the market and the share price takes a long time to recover from such a setback. So always look to ensure that there is an adequate margin to continue to pay the same dividend even if profits do fall—for safetys' sake, see that the dividends do not cost more than 60 per cent of the available earnings. The priority percentages for British Motor Corporation in 1961, for instance, show that Ordinary dividends took from 5-93 per cent of total earnings. Unless earnings rise substantially, there is no chance of a dividend increase and there is the possibility of a cut. Naturally, priority percentages should be looked at in conjunction with the company's gearing (*see* Appendix A).

Sometimes the margin of safety for the Ordinary dividend shown by the priority percentage differs from that shown by the "Times Covered" figure available on the back of the *Financial Times*. These differences are often due to the fact that the *Financial Times* adjusts dividends upwards or downwards according to the most recent interim dividend statement, or adjusts earnings to take into account the effect of investment allowances which increase earnings in earlier years at the expense of later years. They can also be caused by technical factors concerning the actual way in which companies are capitalised. When there are differences play safe. Use the most pessimistic of the two figures. Underneath the priority percentages are the high and low prices of the shares for the last 8 or 9 years. These are not adjusted for capitalisation issues except during the year when it took place and are thus often of no real use.

Balance Sheets and Asset Values

A summary of the balance sheet of the last two or three years is usually given on the back of the card. The actual figures given there are not much use to the investor who does not have the company's accounts, and they should really be ignored. The accounts are extremely important to the investor and they will be touched upon in the next chapter. However, the chairman's report is also précised on the back of the card and this is important to you because it will touch upon such matters as coming "rights" or "capitalisation" issues, the trend of profit margins and, perhaps, the prospects for the coming year.

You will also find some figures underneath the abbreviated balance sheet showing the assets value of the shares and also the net current assets. The net current assets are important because they give some idea of how liquid the company is—that is, whether it is short of money and may need to come to the market to raise more money by a rights issue. The asset value used to be regarded as most important in making up one's mind whether or not to buy a share, but there are one or two disadvantages to this method of investing. In the first place, you want to lend your money to a company that can make use of it and increase its value for you, not one whose only future is liquidation. Look at the management of a company, not at how much its shares might be worth in terms of factories and stocks. Secondly, the figure is extremely tricky to use. Only too often the badly managed company that finds itself in liquidation is the one that discovers on liquidation that its assets are worth much less than the balance sheet figures. The go-ahead company almost certainly underestimates the true value of its assets.

Conclusion

Obviously you do not have to read everything, although the better informed you are the better investor you are likely to be. Probably one of the weekly financial magazines, the City page of your daily newspaper, and the Saturday edition of the *Financial Times*, for its editorials and summary of the week's reports if nothing else, will be sufficient to keep you well informed about the market. However, it is essential that you look into any company that you consider buying. Time skimped here means money lost later. It is also important that you do not allow yourself to be carried away by the mood of the market. The stock market does not react to economic and political factors in a rational way. It has a life of its own. At times the worst possible news has no effect at all; at other times even the most splendid news will make no difference to its depression. Learn to take notice both of the state of the economy and that of the market. Sooner or later the market will adapt itself to the economic facts, and successful investing is the art of being in a position to benefit from this adjustment.

6

CHOOSING YOUR SHARES

There are two common arguments used to justify the
purchase of a share. The more popular and exciting is the
"special situation." It is nearly always the less profitable.
The favourite "special situation" is when you are told, as
you surely will be told, and in confidence of course, that
such and such a company will be taken over in a matter of
time. It hardly ever is. The price falls and you are left
with a bad investment. Another favourite "special
situation" is the "fabulous profits" story. The trouble is
that not only are the profits, however good, never quite
as good as hoped for by the optimists, but the share price
has already fully discounted these good results—and that
accounts for the strange phenomenon of the share price
dropping after the announcement of record results. There
are other "special situation" stories—new management,
return to the dividend list, capital distribution after a
successful sale of some part of the company's land or
plant, enormous new order about to be announced, and so
on—but they all have one thing in common. By the time
you hear about them, the professionals will have acted.
You will be too late to do anything but assure them their
profits by buying the shares they themselves bought days
ago when they were a bargain.

Importance of Management
The other argument for buying a share is management.
This is never such an attractive reason, for very rarely
will you be able to say that a well-managed company is
cheap at the moment and that its price should double over

the next few weeks. But it is the best reason for the long-term investor.

Management is important to the shareholder, and especially the small shareholder with less abillity to keep in close touch with companies than institutional investors. First, good management will take more opportunity of good business conditions, and this will benefit the shareholder in increased dividends. But, more important, good management will mitigate the effects of difficult business conditions and protect the investor from loss of income. Secondly, good management will ensure that the company's resources, as far as possible, are switched to fields where a good return can be earned rather than retained in a sector which is either declining or becoming unprofitable.

There is a third and even more important reason why management matters to the small investor. As I have continually emphasised, investing in equity shares is just one way of hiring out money for an annual return. The full employment policies of governments since the war have resulted in a process of continuous inflation. This has meant that the attractiveness of hiring out capital for a fixed money return, by buying gilt-edged securities or lending money on deposit, has declined in favour of buying something that, by giving an increasing money return, will maintain and perhaps increase the real purchasing power of capital.

Only a few companies in Britain regularly increase their profits and their dividends—far too few, in fact. A little luck and easy business conditions can enable even a badly managed company to produce two or three years of good profits, but only good management will enable a company consistently to do well, irrespective of general economic conditions. The companies that are well managed are continually changing. As companies which have done well in the past grow larger and more cumbersome, and their management less resilient to setbacks and less aware of profitable new openings, their growth characteristics fade away and they are replaced by other, more thrusting companies.

The big insurance companies and pension funds, however, are managed by cautious men—they have to be, for every year commitments have to be met and they cannot afford to take too many chances. It takes a little while, therefore, before the new small companies are accepted as respectable growth stocks and before it is realised that the favourites of previous years have dropped out of the running. The shrewd investor should try to anticipate these changes of opinion. For once the institutions accept a company as a safe growth stock, they begin to buy. And that means that dividend yields drop from about 5 or 6 per cent to 2 or 3 per cent. And the converse happens too.

What is Company Growth?

Unfortunately the management of a company is a most difficult quality to assess. Even if management has been good in the past, there is no indication that it will continue to be good in the future. It may very easily be that as you are considering buying a company, the director who made it what it is is dying or retiring or becoming bored with the company and its problems. But it is worth looking at a company's past record, for that is all the evidence that you will ever have. After all, it is more likely that a company that has done well in the past will continue to do well in the future than that the company with a poor record will suddenly transform itself.

It was said earlier that a more sophisticated economic attitude has allowed governments to protect their peoples from "boom and bust" conditions and that the business cycle is now merely a contrast between different rates of economic advance. The Gross National Product, which is the sum of everything produced by the nation in the course of a year and an indication of its wealth, has risen every year since the war. Since the end of the war, a combination of an increasing population, rising productivity, and inflation has resulted in GNP virtually doubling itself in monetary terms every ten years or so—or a growth at an annual compound rate 6-7 per cent per annum. However, there is no definite relationship between the growth of the economy and the growth of company profits, for while some industries are declining others will be rising and all will be moving at different tempos. The investor will naturally want to choose a field where it is possible for a company to make greater profits every year.

Companies in this country are now required, as they are in America, to disclose their turnover or sales figures. However, this is not as useful as could have been hoped, as larger companies have many different divisions and the individual turnover figures for these divisions are still not disclosed. Moreover, since some divisions are more profitable than others—and some may well be making a loss—it is still difficult to determine, as closely as would be liked, the success of a company. Nevertheless, the combination of total sales figures, together with trading profits does give a reasonable idea of how a company has done. You should expect a company's trading profit to have increased at least as fast as GNP. If it has not, the company is not taking advantage of all the opportunities open. For the company to be described as a growth stock, its trading profits should have increased at least twice as fast as GNP.

Is the Shareholder Benefiting?

The benefits of increased trading must find their way to the shareholder; with poor management these benefits are all too often lost somewhere in the firm. So it is necessary for net profits to show a rise as well. And since any company which is growing should be able to take advantage of some of the "economies of scale"—more work being done by the same number of people, more goods being produced by the same amount of machinery, etc.— net profits should rise a little faster than trading profits.

However, some companies are able to increase their trading and net profits substantially without benefiting the Ordinary shareholder. This is because their expansion is "bought" expansion—the taking-over of other firms is the most obvious example—rather than expansion generated within the firm by greater efficiency and higher utilisation of resources. Earnings per share must show an increase as well, for without that there is no scope for increased dividends and, however great the profit increases, the company will not be a growth stock. Unfortunately, the usual statistical record cards only work out company earnings on the basis of that year's issued Ordinary capital. Because companies increase this over a period of time by the issue of capitalisation shares, these earnings have to be adjusted for all such issues so that the trend of earnings and dividends over a period of years is comparable.

Adjusting Earnings

The following example will show the best way of doing this. Say that a company in year A reports earnings of 50 per cent and pays a dividend of 20 per cent on an issued Ordinary capital of £1 million in £1 shares. It also declares a one for one capitalisation issue. The next year, by some impossible chance, it makes exactly the same profit and pays the same dividend. But this year the earnings and dividend will no longer be 50 per cent and 20 per cent. There is now, after the capitalisation, exactly double the issued capital—£2 million in £1 shares instead of £1 million worth—and this year's earnings are worked out on the increased capital. The earnings will be halved as the capital has been doubled so that earnings are reported as 25 per cent and dividends as 10 per cent.

From a quick glance at the record card, it would appear that the company has done badly because both the earnings and the dividends have been halved. A closer look at the *Exchange Telegraph* card would show that in the dividend column after the dividend figure for year A was "cap 100"; in other words, a 1:1 capitalisation issue. It could have been "cap 50" or a 1:2 free issue, or even "cap 200," a 2:1 capitalisation, or any other figure you care to think of.

In 1963 Imperial Tobacco Company's earnings were 20·2% and the dividend was 10·5%. In that year the company made a 50% scrip issue (1 for 2). In 1964 the earnings were 18·4% and the dividend paid 13·3%. To compare with the 1964 earnings the 1963 earnings must be adjusted for the 50% increase in the capital. The simplest way to do this is to reduce the 1963 figure by a third. So earnings of 20·2% reduced by a third becomes 16·5%. This figure compares with the 18·4% of 1964. The same can be done with the dividend.

Other companies can be adjusted like this. The rule of thumb to remember is to divide the earnings and dividends of previous years by the value of the capitalisation plus 100.

Adjusting earnings for a company like Tesco, which has had five capitalisation issues since 1955, can become a little tedious. However, the easiest way of comparing earnings of 1955 with the most recent figure is this. Under the rule of thumb of adding 100 to the capitalisation figure, the earnings need to be divided by 110 for 1955, 110 for 1956, 130 for 1959, 150 for 1960 and 120 for 1961. If these are multiplied together then (110 × 110 × 130 × 150 ×

120)=283 (ignore the noughts and round off to three figures). 1955 earnings of 63·8 per cent divided by 2·83 gives 22 per cent. 1961 earnings of 65·5 per cent divided by 120 gives 54·5 per cent.

New Exchange Telegraph Cards

Fortunately, the Exchange Telegraph Company now does most of this work for the investor. They produce cards auxiliary to their normal cards (which were described earlier) and these, amongst other things, adjust prices, earnings and dividends for all capitalisation and rights issues. They will also contain priority percentages for the past ten years, the actual earnings on the capital employed in the company, as opposed to the earnings on the company's nominal capital, and a comparison of the yield offered by the company with the yields obtainable on equivalent companies and on the various indices of Ordinary shares. The new card should be used in conjunction with the ordinary one when assessing a company's record and considering its future prospects.

Beware of the company whose earnings growth has slowed down but whose dividend growth is increasing. This process cannot go on for long, and such a company is not a true growth stock.

Other Checks

The statistical record cards will give you the company's records. Your broker will give you the City's opinion of its management and its prospects. Your own knowledge and the reports of consumer magazines like *Which* can sometimes give you an idea of the quality of its products. The financial press should be able to tell you progress of the industry of which the company is a member. A few other simple rules will remove even more of the risk element. Do not buy very small companies. Only stocks with an issued capital of £1 million are considered for trustee buying. This is a little restrictive, for most of the best growth companies are small and growing—by the time they reach the million pound mark the growth has often gone—but do not go below £500,000, and see that the shares are a fairly free market. Your broker will tell you what the market is like on any particular company. Buy only companies with a long and progressive record of profits. Some of these profits may count from the days when the company was private and before it came to the Stock Exchange, but that does not matter. The company to be careful of is the one that suddenly appears from nowhere with fast increasing profits. Often they are "shells" —defunct companies with stock market quotations—or small or near moribund companies that have been taken over and used as a vehicle to bring other small companies to the market. Such industrial holding companies often have an excellent two or three years and a few become large and successful, but most are nothing but a load of junk— and they disappear as soon as the first adverse economic winds blow.

7

HOW AND WHEN TO BUY AND SELL

However careful you are in picking your shares, some risk will still remain. This is why diversification or spreading of risk is so important.

Diversification

Diversification does not mean buying several different companies operating in the same industry. Investors who thought this received a nasty shock when the Hire Purchase bad debts became known, for even the strongest and soundest of the HP companies suffered very badly. Equally it does not mean buying all the shares quoted on the back page of the *Financial Times*. Investing all in one company is gambling in the same way that picking out one horse as a likely winner is gambling; "buying the market" is gambling by betting on all the horses so as not to miss the one which will win. Both types of gambling lose.

Diversification is picking a few good companies from a select list of industries. The amount of money put into each company depends on personal considerations but the principle remains the same—whether £100,000, £10,000 or £1,000. The money is better invested in a dozen or so first class shares than lavishly spread over several score. Obviously the investor with only £100 cannot diversify and would be better advised to buy a trust, but the investor or investment club with £100 coming in every year or every month can diversify over a period of time as a portfolio is built up.

Investment Policy

The alphabetical listing of industrial groups given on the back page of the *Financial Times* is of little use to the investor planning his investment policy. The breakdown used by many brokers is a very much better one:

FINANCE GROUP
  Banks
  Insurance
  Investment Trusts
  Other Financial Companies

METAL AND ENGINEERING GROUP
  Iron and Steel and Non-ferrous Metals
  Non-Electrical Engineering, Shipbuilding, Other Metal Goods
  Vehicles
  Electrical Engineering and Electrical Goods
  Instruments, Jewellery, Precious Metals

OTHER INDUSTRIAL GROUPS
  Chemical and Allied Trades
  Paper, Printing, Publishing
  Building, Contracting and Materials
  Other Manufacturing

CONSUMER TRADES, DISTRIBUTION, SERVICES
  Food, including Distribution
  Drink
  Tobacco
  Cotton
  Wool
  Other Textiles
  Clothing and Footwear Manufacture
  Distribution Services
    Wholesale
    Retail
    Miscellaneous

SHIPPING AND COMMODITIES
  Oil
  Shipping
  Mines and Plantations.

Remember the change in economic conditions when studying this. The policies of the Government have done away with "boom" and "bust" and the business cycle now is the difference between different rates of economic growth. The Government is also committed to full employment and consumer spending should increase to a new record level every year. Finally, as people get richer their needs change from goods to services.

The Service Industries

Because of these factors there are certain industries which should do better year after year—and so should the companies making them up. These companies are mainly those that come under the finance group and consumer trade, although there are exceptions to this ruling, for hire purchase is in the first group and the textile industry in the second and both are cyclical. The rate of profits growth of these companies may vary from one year to another, but it should always be "ever upward." These are the shares to buy first. They should never need to be sold except when the management appears to be weakening or the company getting so large that it begins to suffer from elephantiasis. Then investments should be switched to a more dynamic rival in the same field. Otherwise, they should be held for income and capital growth from one economic crisis to another.

The Cyclical Industries

Once you have built up a portfolio of consumer shares, you can then begin to think of a "second line portfolio" of cyclical shares. The idea here is that you buy them when the price is very low and the outlook is most gloomy and sell them when everyone else is enthusiastic about them. You will soon find that the practical application of this theoretical rule is rather more difficult than it appears at first sight.

Cyclical shares fall into two main categories. Vehicles,

Consumer Durables and Hire Purchase make one grouping. Governments have found these industries very useful scapegoats for their own follies, and investing in these shares, which can be extremely profitable, is complicated by the risk of political action nullifying or exaggerating the usual trade movements. The other cyclical section is composed of Capital Goods shares, i.e., machine tools, heavy engineering, etc. This has been a disappointing section of the market partly because, in many ways, this is the most inefficient and uncompetitive part of British industry, partly because the Government's economic policy since the war has seemed designed to discourage new capital investment. With a capital goods boom only once every five years or so, it is difficult for even highly efficient companies to prosper.

There are finally the shipping, mining and commodity shares. These are for the very expert and the very rich. Both can afford to lose money gaining experience.

Timing

This is the most difficult of stock exchange arts to learn. Few ever succeed in buying at the bottom and selling at the top, but everyone should make an attempt to achieve this ideal. There is certainly no excuse for those investors who consistently buy at the top and sell at the bottom. They have just never bothered to study the market.

The high and low figures given for share prices on the back page of the *Financial Times* clearly show how much prices, even of the best companies, fluctuate in the course of a year. An index in chart form, such as that of the *Financial Times* Index below, shows how markets as a whole fluctuate over a period of time. What is more important, it shows that neither bull markets nor bear markets are consistent. There are always reactions and rallies taking place.

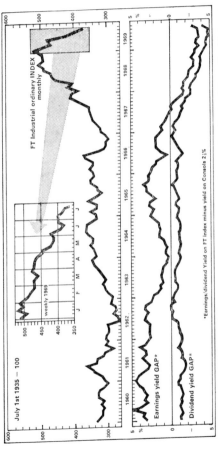

The yield gap is the difference between the averge return that can be obtained from fixed interest government securities, and that which can be obtained from the FT index of ordinary shares. Until the late 50s, an investor always expected to get a lower return from the greater capital safety of a government bond. The change in the past ten years shows how savers now expect inflation to eat away the value of their savings and a fixed interest income, so that they now expect a greater income return from a fixed interest stock than from the more dangerous—in capital terms—ordinary share.

There is a market adage that the soundest way of making money is to buy when everyone else is selling and sell when all are buying. The main objection to this is that stock market primary movements are long term—there was a bull market from the beginning of 1958 to the end of 1959. Anyone following that saying would certainly not have made his fortune. The same is also true of bear markets. The reason that the Wall Street crash is regarded with so much horror is that when many of the professionals moved in early in 1930, thinking that the bear market had bottomed, they were "taken to the cleaners" as thoroughly as the amateur, for prices continued to drop for another two and a half years.

Going Against the Trend

Yet this maxim is certainly true of the rallies and reactions, or secondary movements, that take place during a bear or bull market. The investor should always put himself in a position where he can dictate the terms. This means that shares should not be pushed on to a falling market. Selling is always overdone and sooner or later technical factors will cause a reaction and prices will then move up. That is the time to sell. In the same way do not go chasing shares when prices are booming. Buying will be overdone and there will be a reaction. Once again the investor can step in and buy on his own terms. The important point to remember is that there is no finishing post—except liquidations or bankruptcy—for the horses in the stock exchange race, and bets can be laid all the time. So do not hurry.

Special Situations

"Rights" issues nearly always result in a fall in the company's share price, though often, with a good company, it is only very temporary. Try, however, to take this opportunity to buy, and remember that if you buy "rights" shares nil paid they are not only free of stamp but the brokerage on the premium is very much less than on the fully paid share. "Rights" are often cheapest just after the announcement of the issue and during the first two days of dealing in the Allotment Letters. This is when shareholders are selling their "rights" for the premium. They often weaken again a day or two before the call, as all those shareholders who do not wish to take up their "rights," and speculators in the "rights," then take their last opportunity to sell out. Conversely, these are the worst times to sell.

Keep a close watch on the share prices of companies that take over others for shares. Very often the share price of such a company will be temporarily depressed as the market absorbs large lines of its shares from the former shareholders of the taken-over company. Beware of buying a company just before its results are due, especially if they are expected to be good. The share price discounts this and rather more besides. The results always disappoint the optimists and the share price falls. The converse is often true when poor results are expected. Stock market emotions are always extreme and prices correspondingly reflect this.

Finally, never hang on to a share waiting for a round price. This is sometimes explained as "always leave a bob for the other fellow." Too many investors, if they have a share which they bought at 25s. insist on hanging on for 30s. Unfortunately nearly everyone else is thinking the same way and the price never reaches 30s. Take something less and be done with it. The same goes for buying. If a share is worth buying a few coppers either way will make no difference; if it is worth selling, it should be sold at to-day's price.

Portfolio Management

Investment is not simply picking a share, buying it and then forgetting it. You are buying equity shares for income and capital growth. In order to obtain the best returns you will have to follow your investments and make changes in your portfolio. In particular there will be times when you have to decide whether to take profits or losses on certain of your shares.

The professional's rule of action is to "run profits and cut losses." This is a rule that is ideal for the short-term speculator. It needs to be modified for the long-term investor.

You should run your profits like the professional. Never sell a share because the price looks too high. Only sell it when you think the company's future is no longer attractive and it seems that profits will stop growing. Never sell a good share simply because it has gone up in price and you can realise a profit. When you have to sell to realise some cash, always pick the weakest share in your portfolio. This usually means the one that has disappointed and has shown little or no growth or even a capital loss. Too many investors practise a form of negative selectivity. They always sell the share that does well and hold those that have done badly. The money realised is reinvested and the process continues. The end result is a portfolio of bad shares with not one likely growth stock among them. This is the sort of investor who wonders why he does so badly. He would certainly be better off in a building society or the Port Office Savings Bank.

The investor must, however, be careful about needlessly cutting losses. There are two types of losses on the stock exchange. There is the "book" loss when a share is standing at a lower price than that at which you bought it. Theoretically, you are losing money on it. But you don't actually lose anything until you sell the share. That is when you "realise" your loss. Naturally, the same is true of profits.

Cutting Losses

Sometimes you must realise your book losses. You might not have investigated the company and its affairs as closely as you ought to have done, some news might come out which casts considerable doubt on the company's future prospects, or you might hear that the dividend is likely to be cut. In such cases "first loss" is often "least loss." But remember this: you not only take the loss caused by the fall in share price but you probably lose the dividend and, as well, have to meet buying and selling expenses. On top of that you will have buying expenses on the next share you buy. Until the price of that appreciates sufficiently to compensate for the loss and the expenses, your investment policy is not successful. Think hard before buying a share; think even harder before selling it at a loss; and always remember the tax angle.

Averaging

It is more likely that a book loss is the result of buying at the top of a speculative wave of buying. In this case you have two choices. Either the shares can be held for recovery—and if the company is sound they will recover—or more can be bought as an averaging purchase. The principle behind averaging is simple. If a share at 40s. is attractive, it is more attractive at 30s.—all other things being equal. This low price allows a further purchase. The actual book loss sustained on the total investment remains the same but the book price of the individual share is brought down so that a relatively smaller rise in the share price is needed to convert a book loss into a book profit. 200 shares bought at 40s. would cost, disregarding expenses, £400. If the share price drops to 30s. the value of the holding will drop to £300, a book loss of 10s. per share or £100. Another 200 shares bought at 30s. would bring the total holding to 400 shares costing £700. The total book loss would still be the same for the market value would only be £600, but the book loss per share would now only be 5s., i.e., £700 for 400 shares = 35s. a share. Taking up rights issues and applying for excess rights also helps to bring down the book value of a share.

The converse can also be done by selling some shares off at a high price and thus bringing down the book cost of the remainder. A good example of both types of averaging is given below.

CEMENTATION 4s. SHARES
Bought

			£	s.	d.
Nov.	600 Shares:	Original cost	264	1	2
Feb.	200 Shares:	Rights @ 8s.	80	0	0
Feb.	200 Shares:	Excess Rights @ 8s.	80	0	0
Jan.	500 Shares:	Rights @ 6s. 3d.	156	5	0
Jan.	45 Shares:	Excess Rights @ 6s. 3d.	14	1	3
	1,545		£594	7	5

Sold

		£	s.	d.
Dec.	545 @ 10s. 10½d.	296	6	10½
Aug.	1,000 @ 12s. 4½d.	618	15	0
	1,545	£915	1	10½

Two things should be noticed from this example. One was that no pretence was made to buy or sell at the top and bottom of the market. However, the taking up of rights and excess rights effectively reduced the book cost of the shares. This could also have been done through an averaging purchase. Also, by never selling when his shares were showing a book loss, this investor received £109 in dividends. The second point is the precautionary sale of 545 shares. This brought the book cost of the remaining 1,000 shares down to 6s. 1d. per share. He later sold the remainder for 12s. 4½d. But had he not done so, the first sale would still have minimised the loss that he would have seen when, in 1960, the company passed its dividend and the share price fell from a high of 15s. to 5s.

There are objections to averaging. All too often investors try to average far too quickly and thus buy for a second time well above the share's low. They are often unselective and average in poor shares when the money would be far better employed in a different company and perhaps a different industry. This is often true but it does not have to be so. The small investor would do far better to emulate the jobber and follow a few select shares. He will then be able to take advantage of the fluctuation in share prices of about 40% or so in a year and average in his shares when the price is low and sell out when it is high. And by restricting his choice to a few growth stocks, he eliminates the risk of pouring good money after bad. There is an objection to partial sales. It is said that if some shares should be sold, then all should be sold; if some held, all held. This is true enough for the professional but the average investor is pretty cautious. Partial sales allow him to have his cake and eat it too. The total size of the cake may be slightly smaller; on the other hand, there is a much smaller risk of it disappearing altogether.

Investment Systems

Investors have always been fascinated by the thought of a "system" that would take them into the markets at the bottom and out at the top. Before the war there was a case for basing such a system on the business cycle. The expert on this—L. L. B. Angas of *Investment*—found that between 1801 and 1928 there were definite cycles in security prices of approximately eight years. The time was long enough, and the price movements wide enough, to make it worth while switching from equities to gilts over this cycle. Unfortunately, the researches of both Angas and Keynes were published at about the same time—and Keynesian methods of economic controls have put paid to Angas's methods of investment.

Nevertheless, investors are still seeking systems. Most are now based on the movements of various charts which can be made of stock exchange price movements, yields, and activity. But economic policy becomes less and less austerely monetary and impartial and more and more political and planned. Charts lump all the sectors of the market together—those industries adversely affected by the government's economic policies, those unaffected and those which benefit. In present day circumstances buying and selling the market is pointless. Charts can show the general mood of sentiment—and anyone who invests without knowing whether the market is in a bull or bear phase is stupid—but charts will not show which way individual share prices will move any more. More than ever before, money can still be made in bear markets. As the American broker says, you just have to be selective and, by selective, we mean buying only those shares which go up.

8

THE TAXMAN COMETH

The taxman always comes, of course; it is just that he
has been coming more frequently and in a more complicated fashion since the election of the Labour Government
in 1964.

Corporation Tax

Until the 1965 Budget, companies in Britain were regarded, for tax purposes, as equivalent to individual per-
sons. Excluding taxation allowances granted to companies, every £1 of profits that a company made was taxed,
just like an individual, at 8s. 3d.; also it had to pay
an additional 3s. profit tax. The remaining 8s. 9d. was "net
profit" and could be distributed to shareholders or kept
in the company without further payment of tax. So a
company earning £100 would pay £41 5s. income tax and
£15 profit tax and have a net profit of £43 15s. If the company paid a dividend of £21 17s, 6d. this would be described as a "twice covered" dividend. In other words,
both the company and the individual had the same interest
as tax was only paid once on profits, whether paid out as
dividends or retained within the company to pay for its
further expansion.

This has now changed and companies are regarded as
quite separate entities for tax purposes. As from 1st April,
1968, the same company earning £100 profit pays Corporation Tax of 45% i.e., £45. (The rate started off at 40%
and seems likely to go higher.) This means the company
has £55 profit after tax from which to pay a dividend. But
any part of this paid out as a dividend has to have income

tax deducted from it, i.e., a further 8s. 3d. in the £1. So, if the company wishes its shareholders to continue to get a net dividend of nearly £22—as in the earlier case—it will actually have to pay out over £36 from its profit of £55, i.e., £14 17s. to the Revenue with income tax at 8s. 3d. and £21 3s. to its shareholders. This means the company will keep only £79 of its profits for its further expansion— and the higher the dividend, the less it keeps. The converse, of course, is that if it pays nothing to shareholders, it will keep more of its profit for future expansion than under the old system.

Whatever the advantages or disadvantages of Corporation Tax, it has undoubtedly simplified life for the investment analyst. The old complicated system of "grossing up" and "netting down" to get "earnings per share" has now gone. The "earnings" of a company—or the net amount of money a company has to pay dividends to its shareholders—is now simply the profits left after paying Corporation Tax and any dividends on preference shares that the company has in issue. These "earnings" can easily be expressed as a percentage of the total ordinary capital of the company. The company mentioned above making £55 after Corporation Tax might have a capital of £100 divided into 100 £1 shares. Earnings are 55% on this basis and "earnings per share" are 11s. (55% of £1=11s.) If the price in the stock market of the £1 share was 77s., this would give a Price Earnings Ratio of 7 (77s. divided by 11s.) and the PER is one of the basic measuring devices of the analyst.

Short-Term Gains Tax

This tax was, and is, designed to discourage short-term dealing in the Stock Exchange. If you buy a share and sell it at a profit within 12 months of purchase, then that capital profit will be regarded as unearned income and will be taxed at your top rate of taxation and surtax, where it applies. For most investors, this will be at least 8s. 3d. in the £1, and for many others, considerably higher.

The Long-Term Gains Tax

This tax applies to all capital gains realised on the sale of a security that has been held for a period of more than 12 months. It is charged at the rate of 30% or alternatively, where beneficial, 50% of the gain up to £5,000 (i.e. £2,500) is treated as income subject to income tax and surtax. When shares are inherited and then are sold again within 12 months any gain which is realised is subject to Long-Term Gains Tax and not Short-Term Gains Tax.

What is a Gain?

The rule for both long- and short-term gains tax is that the gain—or loss—is the difference between the cost of the security plus all expenses such as stamp duty, registration fees and commissions to stockbrokers and the net proceeds from the sale, which again allows for Stock Exchange brokerage.

What is a Net Gain?

Tax, whether short or long term, is only levied on the net gain. Net gains in any year of under £50 are not subject to capital gains tax. Losses on shares can be offset against profits but, and this is important, only short-term losses can be offset against short-term profits and only long-term losses can be set against long-term profits. However, losses, whether long or short term, can be carried forward indefinitely to be offset against future profits, if there are not sufficient allowable profits in the year that the losses are realised.

What is a Realisation?

A realisation for gains tax purposes is the sale of shares for cash. This does not have to be a voluntary sale. If company A takes over company B by a cash offer, this is a realisation and you must pay gains tax on any profit. If, however, company A takes over company B by an offer of its shares, for tax purposes this is not a realisation until you sell the company A shares.

How to Keep the Gains Tax to a Minimum

No one wants to pay more tax than is absolutely necessary. Ideally, you will never take a profit under 12 months and only rarely sell shares over 12 months. But this is not an ideal world. On death the long-term tax of 30% on gains realised in excess of £5,000 will have to be paid anyway, and before that happens, you will quite certainly buy some shares that are disappointing performers. The gains tax reinforces the Stock Exchange maxim of "running profits and cutting losses." If your shares are performing well, hold on to them and don't sell. But where they are performing badly, or things have gone awry since you bought, then sell. Take the profit, if there is one, or more likely the loss, and buy something else. And if you don't have a profit to offset against the loss, don't worry. The loss can be carried forward, and one day that will be useful when you have to take a profit. This is all the more true of the short-term gains tax with its much higher tax rate, and, in the end, a taxable gain is still better than no gain at all or else a loss, because you held on to your shares too long and failed to take your profit.

Tax Relief on Bank Interest

Until the 1969 Budget, it was possible to borrow money from a bank or stockbroker and claim the interest payments on the borrowed money against income tax. This can now only be done when the money is borrowed in order to buy a house. But a company can still claim relief on interest payments. Because of this it has become even more worthwhile, if you do sufficient dealing on the Stock Exchange, to set up an investment dealing company. This can borrow money to buy shares and claim relief; in addition, it gives much greater freedom of buying and selling. It will have to pay Corporation Tax at 45% on its net profits from dealing in shares, but though this is higher than the individual's rate of 30% on long-term gains, it is cheaper than the individual's short term-rate. And you will be able to claim some of the net profit of the company as "earned income" in the shape of director's fees.

A Child's Guide

Capital gains tax is fiendishly complicated in its detail, and the Inland Revenue has produced a "Child's Guide" to capital gains tax (143 pages and an index of 8 pages, free from your local inspector of taxes). It is a wise child indeed who will understand it.

9

THROUGH THE LETTERBOX

Once you become a shareholder, you can begin to expect an interesting mail.

Dividends

The first and most pleasant thing that you are likely to receive is your dividend. This consists of a dividend warrant, stating the amount of dividend due to you, the amount of tax deducted and the cheque for the net amount of dividend. You can immediately cash the dividend. The dividend warrant you should keep. If you pay less than the standard rate of tax, i.e., you do not pay 8s.3d. in the £ on any of your income, then at the end of the year you can return the dividend warrant with your income tax return and claim for a return of some or all of the tax paid by the company on your behalf. If you are lucky enough to pay surtax, i.e., you earn over £5,000 a year, then you will also have to return your dividend warrant— not to reclaim tax but to pay more.

Double Tax Relief

There is one important proviso to all this. The Inland Revenue authorities, despite popular belief to the contrary, are a fair-minded body and they do not wish to tax the same income twice. However, when British companies have subsidiaries operating overseas, it is possible that the profits made by those companies are taxed both by the government of the country in which they operate and by the revenue authorities here when these profits are remitted to the parent company. To avoid such inequities, the authorities enter into double tax agreements with overseas governments. The effect of these is to ensure that companies are taxed only once. The governments concerned decide how they will divide the taxes between them.

Accounts

The next document you receive will be less welcome than the dividend, but much more important. It is the company's accounts. These give a financial X-ray of the company's state of health, showing up weaknesses and strengths and sometimes, in conjunction with other and more general information, showing how well it is doing.

There are two important tables in the accounts. One is the consolidated profit and loss account, the same figures as are summarised on the statistical record card and which show the success of the company and its associated companies over the past year. The other is the consolidated balance sheet, the statement of the financial position of the company and its associates at one particular moment of time—the end of its financial year. It is idle to pretend that company accounts are easy to understand. But they can be mastered, especially with the help of the books mentioned in the bibliography, and they must be mastered by anyone who intends to take investment seriously.

The Chairman's Statement

The accounts generally contain the chairman's yearly report. This is compulsory reading for everyone. These reports and the company's record can give a good idea of whether the company's management is up to its job, what the past year has been like, and what the future holds.

Proxies

Most accounts will usually include a pre-paid proxy card. This invites you to nominate someone to vote on your behalf on the resolutions to be put before the company meeting. You can either nominate one of the directors listed on the form, and indicate which way you want him to vote, or you can nominate someone else entirely—and he or she does not have to be a shareholder. If you can go to the company meeting though, you ought to, and it does not matter if you have already nominated a proxy. The tone of the meeting will tell you a lot about the company. People only turn up and start asking awkward questions when things are going wrong. But look at the directors as well and ask yourself whether they impress you. A great number of people I know have bought and sold shares in a company because of the impression made upon them by the Board. They have been remarkably successful investors too.

Capitalisation and Rights Issues
If you receive something called an Allotment Letter, you will know that your company is making a capitalisation issue—the official name for something which is often called a "scrip," "free" or "bonus" issue—or a rights issue. The Allotment Letter will announce along the top that "this is a valuable document and if you do not know what to do with it immediately approach your stockbroker or banker."

Allotment Letters are negotiable instruments. That is, they can be bought and sold and possession of a correctly renounced Allotment Letter establishes the purchaser's rights to whatever benefits it may confer. Dealings in Allotment Letters on the stock exchange normally begin the day you receive them and they generally continue for between 4 and 6 weeks. Further, since the purchase of an Allotment Letter establishes your claim to the ownership of the "new" shares rather than merely transferring something already in existence, the Government's 2 per cent stamp duty is not levied on these deals.

There is a simple reason for the issue and use of Allotment Letters. New issues are made in proportion to existing holdings, i.e., one or part of one new share for every old share held. This results in investors finding themselves with an odd or "broken" number of shares. Some investors, particularly the institutions, do not like this. They therefore either buy more or sell some so that they can round off their holdings. Again, not all investors can afford to take up a "rights" issue and so they must either sell all of them or sufficient of them to take up the remainder. If the company had to register all these transactions and issue share certificates for them, it would be an intolerable burden. As it is, the Allotment Letter system allows investors to settle the matter among themselves, so that by the time the company comes to register the new shareholders the market has settled down.

Capitalisation Issues

(*Known also as "Free," "Bonus" or "Scrip" Issues.*)
There is nothing "free" about a free issue: it is merely a book-keeping transaction, and the nearest analogy to a 1 for 1 capitalisation is the exchange of £1 for two 10s. notes. Capitalisation refers to capitalisation of reserves. These reserves come from profits which the shareholders have not received as dividends but which have been ploughed back into the business instead.

The law makes it necessary for companies to issue shares of a specific par or nominal value. This means that a company's capital is also quoted as a fixed and unchanging sum. Over a period of time this nominal value loses all relation to the actual value of the company's capital which is continually being enlarged by ploughing back profits and the inflationary increase of assets' value. But the earnings and dividend figures continue to be quoted as a percentage of the nominal value. There are political and industrial disadvantages to reporting earnings of 200 per cent or dividends of 100 per cent of the nominal value of a share. And so companies find it convenient to capitalise their reserves and increase the number of shares and thus the company's nominal capital. The same dividend is paid but over a larger number of shares and thus the lower dividend percentage figures reported go unremarked.

A good example of this was the Rhokana Corporation capitalisation issue in 1959. In that year the company reported earnings of 357·8 per cent and a dividend of 320 per cent. Such figures could scarcely be described as politically popular. The following year, earnings of 73·6 per cent and a dividend of 56 per cent were declared. These figures were still high but not nearly so unpopular. In fact, 1960 figures were nearly double those of 1959. The company had a 9 for 1 capitalisation in 1959—shareholders ended up by having 10 shares where previously they only had one. Adjusted for this, earnings in 1959 were only 35·8 per cent and the dividend was 32 per cent. In other words, Rhokana shareholders both kept their cake and ate it: the dividend was nearly doubled and they escaped the odium of "high" percentage figures.

The simplest way of calculating the value of the capitalisation issue, and thus the value of the old shares ex the issue, is to take the cost of the number of old shares needed to obtain one new share and divide the cost by the increased number of shares. In the case of a one to one capitalisation:

1 old share @ 40s.
1 new share @ ——

total cost of 2 shares = 40s.
Each share ex-capitalisation = 20s.

If the capitalisation issue were a one to three, the method would be much the same:

3 old shares @ 40s. each = 120s.
1 new share @ ———

_____

total cost of 4 shares = 120s.
Each share ex-capitalisation = 30s.

The difference between the old price—40s.—and the ex-capitalisation price—30s.—is the amount by which the share price on the old share will drop when trading in the new shares commences. Theoretically, shareholders neither gain nor lose. They just have more shares at a lower price.

Why "Free Issues" are Popular

Quite often the price of a company's shares after a capitalisation issue stands higher than it ought to be theoretically. It is this that helps to foster the illusion that shareholders are getting something for nothing. The higher price is usually due to the market's belief that a Board which makes a scrip issue is confident of the company's future and to the hope that the effective dividend rate will be raised—sometimes by paying the same percentage rate on the increased capital. Companies often announce that they will do this at the same time as making the issue. But the share price rises because of the actual or expected increase in the dividend payment, not because of the scrip issue. If you sell your new shares, you are reducing your proportionate stake in the company. If you spend the proceeds, you are consuming capital, that is, spending your savings.

"Scrip" versus "Rights" Allotment Letters

An Allotment Letter for a "rights" issue is a much more important document than one for a capitalisation. If you do nothing with your capitalisation Allotment Letter you will lose nothing, for in due course the company will send you your new share certificate. If you do nothing with your "rights" letter, you will lose money. So it is important to recognise the difference. Both are generally called Allotment Letters. The scrip Allotment Letter is normally called a "fully paid Allotment or Acceptance Letter." It will tell you the number of shares to which you are entitled, but it will not ask for money. The "rights" issue letter will be headed "provisional Allotment Letter" and will tell you the number of shares to which you are entitled, the cost per share and the total amount that you must send to the company's bankers and the last date on which your application will be accepted. If you neither sell nor accept your rights, you will lose money.

"Rights Issues"

Say that you are a shareholder in a company whose nominal capital is £1 million in the form of 2 million Ordinary shares of 10s. each. The present price of the 10s. shares is 30s. The company wants to raise another £1¼ million to expand its business. It could do so by issuing 2½ million new shares at 10s. each. It could equally well do so by issuing about 834,000 new shares at 30s. each. The company wants the money and does not want the issue to be spurned by its shareholders. The company's bankers do not want to lose face by making an issue which is not a success. So the price decided on is one which raises as much money per share as possible and yet remains attractive to shareholders. In this case the issue would be one new share at 25s. for every two shares held.

The Need to Take Up "Rights"

If the general public were allowed to get these new shares at 25s., existing shareholders would be rather annoyed. Their equity would be diluted, for others would be able to get for 25s. the benefits of being a shareholder in this particular company which had cost existing shareholders 30s. And so "rights" issues are made only on a strictly proportional basis to existing shareholders. This is also the reason why you should take up your "rights." It is virtually impossible to measure what the Ordinary shareholder of a company owns since Ordinary shareholders own "the equity" or everything after all prior charges have been met. What is certain is that if you hold 60 shares in this particular company then you own 60/2,000,000th or 3/100,000th of its equity. If you take up your "rights" you will continue to own 3/100,000th (90/3,000,000th). If you don't take them up, your holding will fall to 60/3,000,000th, or a mere 2/100,000th.

Calculating the Value of "Rights"

The calculation of the value of the "rights" is quite simple. As it is a 1 for 2 rights issue:

```
2 old shares @ 30s. =60s.
1 new share  @ 25s. = 25s.
_____
total of 3 shares =85s.
Each share ex-rights = 28s. 4d.
```

This is the price to which the old shares will fall when they go ex-rights. The value of the "rights" is 30s.—28s. 4d.= 1s. 8d. per share, and as 2 shares are needed to acquire a right to 1 new share, the premium on the new shares will be 1s. 8d. × 2=3s. 4d. This is the price the general public will have to pay to be allowed to take up any of the new shares and also the price you will get for your "rights" shares if you decide to sell them. Of course, prices are fluctuating from day to day and so will the value of these "rights." This value is generally referred to as the "premium." Not everyone can take up "rights" issues, especially if they have no available cash, and the best thing to do is to sell sufficient of the "rights" at a premium to be able to accept the remainder. Your stockbroker will tell you how many you need to sell. But if you spend the premium, you are consuming capital again.

Where the Value Lies

There is one important point about "rights" issues which you ought to realise. The benefit of a "rights" issue to you is not the "bonus" element in the price or the difference in price between the old shares and the price of the new. It is the profit and dividend announcement made by the company at the time of the issue. If it says that it will pay the same rate of dividend on the increased capital, this is equivalent to an increased dividend on the old capital. But, especially if the "rights" issue is offered at a much lower price than the existing market price of the shares, the dividend may be scaled down to take this into account. The real benefit of a "rights" issue is shown by the difference between the dividend yield on the old shares before the "rights" announcement and the yield on the old shares ex-rights on the new dividend forecast.

The Mechanics of Allotment Letters

There are five important dates in your rights letter. The first is the last day for "renunciation and part splitting" of your rights in a "nil paid" form. If you do not want to take up your rights, or wish to sell some to raise the money to take up the remainder, you must sell your rights on the market at a premium and renounce your rights on the back of the Allotment Letter. If you sell only some of them, then you renounce these and send the Allotment Letter to the issuing house, who will split it into two or more Allotment Letters and return them to the various owners. The premium on the new shares is generally depressed during the first two or three days of dealing, when many people are selling, and the last two days or so before acceptance day. Try to sell some time between these two periods. The next date is "acceptance day," by which time the rights must have been paid for. If you are on holiday, see that someone is looking after your shares for you. Dealings continue in the "fully paid Allotment Letters," still without incurring stamp duty, and the next date is "renunciation and part-splitting fully paid." This is for the same purpose as in the "nil-paid form." About two days later comes "renunciation and registration." This is the last day for selling or buying without paying stamp duty, and after that the name of the new shareholder is put on the company's register. After this day also, the financial papers cease to quote two classes of share, the old and the "new," and only one price quotation is made for all shares. Finally, there is the date when you send off the Allotment Letter to the company and receive your share certificate in exchange.

Trading Cum and Ex

Trading in shares goes on continuously, and so companies, because of the administrative problems involved in paying dividends or sending out Allotment Letters, have to draw a line at a certain date. Shareholders registered before then are sent the dividend and Allotment Letters: those not registered by then are not. However, what suits the company does not necessarily suit the Stock Exchange, and so the Council of the Stock Exchange also draws the line. Those who buy shares before this buy "cum" the dividend or issue or whatever; those who buy after buy "ex." From your point of view it is the Council's ruling which is important, not the company's.

Shares go ex-dividend (xd) on the first day of normal trading of the account before the one in which the company "closes its books," i.e., draws the line and says that only shareholders registered by then shall receive the dividend. Theoretically, the price of the share should fall by the net amount of the dividend on the day it goes xd. The shares then are quoted in the newspapers for the remainder of the account as xd. If you sell the shares before they go xd, you may quite easily receive a dividend from the company but it is not yours and, sooner or later, your broker will ask for it.

The object of this is to save the broker and the company the tremendous amount of work that would be involved if shares were traded cum-dividend up to the time that the Annual General Meeting ratifies the size of the dividend. It seems strange that shares should go xd long before the dividend is ratified by the shareholders but, since this is a mere formality, it does not matter greatly.

Shares go ex-capitalisation (xc) or ex-rights (xr) on the day that dealings begin in the Allotment Letter. Here again, though you sell cum-capitalisation or cum-rights, you may receive the Allotment Letter. It is not yours, and you must pass it on to your broker. An important point for buyers to remember is this. If you buy shares cum-capitalisation or cum-rights, after the company has closed its books, it is your responsibility to ask your broker to claim the Allotment Letter for you from the seller. Again, your shares are generally quoted xc or xr for the period of the account during which they went ex.

Excess Rights

A rights letter will often be accompanied by a form of application for excess rights. This is not a negotiable document since no value can be put to it, for no one can know in advance how many shareholders will not take up their rights and how many shareholders will apply for the excess shares. However, if the rights go to a premium there is obviously point in applying for excess shares, even if only to sell them immediately on receipt. It is a condition with excess shares that only shareholders on the register at the appropriate time can apply for them. If you are not on the register, and even though you bought cum-rights, you cannot apply for excess shares. You can ask the seller to apply for you, but he is under no obligation to do so and he may decide to apply on his own behalf even though he is not entitled to the rights issue as such.

New Issues

The most attractive method of buying a company is often when it is first introduced to the stock market. Although there are four methods by which companies are sold to the public, these methods break down into two main headings and it is really only the first heading which affects the average investor.

Offers for Sale and Prospectus Offers

There are theoretical differences between these two methods of bringing companies to the market but they do not affect the investor. Both involve a full page advertise-ment in two national papers, one of which is nearly always the *Financial Times*. These advertisements contain full details of the company's history and particularly its financial record, a description of what it does and a balance sheet attested by the company's accountants. It also includes a form at the bottom inviting investors to apply for shares at a fixed price.

The attraction of this method is that, as a new company, the price at which the shares are offered must be more attractive than the price at which equivalent companies are selling. If the company is attractive—and it should be assessed in the same way as any other company, by looking at its record—the share is likely to go to a premium as soon as dealings begin. Furthermore, there is no stamp duty during the first few weeks of dealings in the new shares and, on application, no brokerage need be paid.

In a bull market there are generally many more applications than shares available and quite often the company has to ballot or scale down applications. Nevertheless, although the investor who applies for only about 200 shares may often be unlucky in the ballot, it is always worth applying for the shares. After all it only costs a 5d. stamp and a cheque form. The *Financial Times* always has a full analysis of the company coming to the market at the same time as the issue is advertised. The sort of things to beware of are profits that, after many years of doing nothing, suddenly jump substantially, and of management which appears to be selling out completely. What the *Financial Times* can say is restrained by the laws of libel, but they can always imply whether they think it is an issue worth going for or not. It is worth following their advice; some issues do go to a discount!

Tenders

There is another variant of the offer for sale which has become popular, particularly when the company coming to the stock market is unique or is a service company with few assets, or has some other peculiarity which makes its price difficult to determine. This is known as an offer by tender. Instead of asking investors to offer to buy the company's shares at a fixed price, as in an offer for sale, the issuing house asks investors to tender for shares at any price above a certain minimum. In other words, the issuing house says that they feel the company's shares are worth at least 14s.—which is the *minimum* tender price— but invite investors to tender for these shares at anything above 14s., though generally in multiples of 6d., that they think justified. As a private investor it is important to follow the informed press. They generally have a good idea of the level at which tenders will be successful—i.e., how much more than 14s. a share you should offer in order to get an allotment of the shares. Do not tender at a ridiculous price above the minimum price of 14s. to make sure of getting some shares. If many investors do this—as has happened with certain issues—the issue may be so over-priced that the shares go to a discount on the agreed price as soon as dealings open. This is a painful way of becoming "a stag."

Placings and Introductions

Advertisements have to be placed in national papers for either a placing or an introduction but these advertisements do not contain a form of application for the shares. With a placing, shares are made available through the jobbers and the issuing house to whoever wants them. Since the price can again be expected to go to a premium, there is generally no shortage of applicants, and, although you can ask your broker to apply for shares, you should not be too downhearted if you never get them. With an introduction, no new capital is being raised, but shares which have been in existence privately are publicly traded for the first time. Once again, sufficient shares are made available to the jobbers to make a market. Both these methods of introducing companies to the stock exchange are very much cheaper than public offers for sale or a prospectus issue, and this is the reason for their popularity.

10

THE ZOO

Earlier I said that there were hundreds of technicalities concerned with the Stock Exchange Account. The most important of these, of course, is that shares bought during an account do not have to be paid for until settlement day, eleven days after the end of that Account. Conversely, shares sold during an account do not have to be delivered until settlement day either. Another important technicality, at any rate to the speculator, is the fact that if shares are bought and sold within an account, then no transfer stamp and fee is payable while the broker, at his discretion, can charge only one commission on the two deals. This, of course, brings down dealing expenses tremendously.

The attraction of this type of speculation is enhanced by "new time" dealing. During the last two business days of an account, shares can be bought, at a small premium, for New Time. This means that the transaction is regarded as falling into the following account and thus the speculator gains an extra two days for the period in which he can deal without incurring stamp duty.

Bulls

A Bull is someone who thinks prices will rise and therefore buys a share, intending to sell it at a profit before settlement day comes and he has to pay for it. More generally, it means investors who are optimistic about the course of share prices. As a result, a rising market is often called a "bull market."

Bears

A Bear is the opposite of a bull. He is someone who sells shares, which he does not own, hoping that the price will fall before settlement day. If prices do fall, he is able to buy in the shares that he has already sold at a lower price than that which he received for them. The difference is his profit. A "covered bear" is someone who sells shares that he does in fact own but who hopes that prices will fall sufficiently for him to be able to buy more shares to deliver, rather than delivering those that he already owns. Since prices could rise indefinitely, the loss that a bear faces could be infinite. By "covering" himself, a bear is restricting his possible loss. More generally, a bear refers to someone who is pessimistic about the likely trend of share prices and, from this, is used to denote a falling market.

Contangoes

Bulls and bears do not always succeed in judging the market correctly. So they sometimes need to defer payment for the shares or delivery of them until after settlement day. This can be done, at a price, and only in active stocks. A contango, sometimes known as a continuation or carry-over, is an arrangement whereby someone who has bought shares and does not wish to pay for them, comes to an agreement with someone who is due to deliver the same number of shares to defer payment. The person who is deferring his purchase is known as the "giver" since he has to pay interest to the "taker," the person agreeing to defer his delivery of shares. Since "takers" and "givers" must be matched, contangoes can only be arranged in stocks with a large and very active market. Very occasionally, the number of people wishing to defer payment is equal to those wishing to defer delivery and then no interest is payable by the "giver." Even more rarely, "takers" predominate and must induce buyers to defer purchase by giving an agreed amount of money per share.

The effect of a contango is to allow a transaction carried out in one account to be transferred to another, and yet another if necessary, without incurring stamp duty or the need to pay for or deliver shares. Brokers do not charge commission on contangoes but remunerate themselves by charging the "giver" a slightly higher rate of interest than they themselves have to pay the market to arrange the contango. Many brokers regard contangoes as outright speculation and so avoid them.

Options

Option dealing is another out and out method of speculating. Theoretically, it minimises possible losses; in fact, it is often used by those with insufficient capital to buy shares, and maximises losses.

The principle of an option is simple. If there is a share now standing at 25s. and you think it is possible that it will go to 35s. but cannot afford to buy the shares, then you can take out a "call option." This is the right to buy the shares at a negotiated price any time over the next three months. There are options of one or two months' duration, but since the price is little different from a three months option, they are fairly rare. The price at which you can call the share is called the "striking price" and is usually about 2 per cent above to-day's buying price. The option itself will cost money, the amount depending on how actively the stock is traded and the market's views as to future price movements. There will also be the normal dealing expenses. The share price will need to rise by at least 10 per cent before there is the chance of a profit.

However, assuming the price does rise, then the procedure is that on any "declaration day" over the next three months, i.e., the penultimate dealing day in the account, you can call your option and then sell your shares. And there is your profit.

A "put option" is the same thing but the other way round. This option allows you to sell shares some time in the future at to-day's price. The negotiated price with a "put option" is generally to-day's selling price. If you declare your option and immediately buy shares in the market to cover delivery, once again you have realised a profit. It is also possible to buy a "put and call option." The cost is double that of a one-way option.

If prices do not move as expected, then everything is lost. By buying the shares, you at least have something left whatever happens to the price. If you do hold shares, and see a great deal of option activity in that company, do not be alarmed. It is almost certainly stock exchange clerks gambling on baseless rumours.

Stags

In favourable market conditions, new issues nearly always go to a premium—i.e., rise above the introduction price. Stags are people who apply for these new shares intending to sell them immediately they are received. Since most issuing houses do not bother to present cheques sent in with application forms, this is a cheap method of gambling. If a particular application is lucky and the cheque is presented for payment, this can immediately be covered by selling the shares received and remitting the cash to the bank. Of course, bank managers do not like this. Even more important, issues have been known to go to a discount, even in the most buoyant of bull markets, and then it is not so easy to cover the cheque. Bank managers like this even less.

All these methods are excellent ways of making money. There are even better methods of losing it. Investors should know them, but they should have nothing to do with them.

APPENDIX A

Gearing

Nearly all companies are geared. In financial parlance, gearing is the term used to describe the relation between the capital of a company that earns itself a fixed rate of return and the risk-bearing capital that earns a variable rate—in general, the Ordinary capital.

It can be assumed that all the capital in a company is earning the same rate of return. If a company's gearing is high, this means that a given rise in the rate of return on capital—i.e., a rise in profits—will lead to a more than proportionate increase in the profits available for the Ordinary shareholder. This is best explained by an example.

Rank Organisation has fairly high gearing. Between 1959 and 1960 the total net earnings of the company rose by 59 per cent—from £813,000 to £1,290,000.

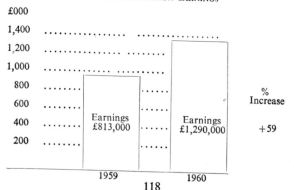

RANK ORGANISATION EARNINGS

£000

1,400 ······

1,200 ······

1,000 ······

800 ······   Earnings £813,000

600 ······

400 ······   Earnings £1,290,000   % Increase

200 ······   +59

        1959   1960

118

But the Ordinary shareholder did rather better than this. The reason being that in both years the prior charge holders only took the same absolute amount in dividends—slightly less in 1960 because of the operation of the sinking fund which reduces the debenture and loan stocks—but in 1960 this was a much smaller proportionate amount of the total available for distribution.

RANK ORGANISATION EARNINGS

£000

£000					
1,400	....				
1,200	....				% Increase in Earnings for Ordinary
1,000	....				
800	......		....	Earned for Ordinary	
600	Priority % 25-100	Earned for Ordinary £618,000	Priority % 16-100	Ordinary £1,101,000	+77
400					
200	......		....		
	0-24	Prior Charges £195,000	0-15	Prior Charges £189,000	

Of course, exactly the same thing can happen in reverse; it is unwise to be in highly geared companies in cyclical industries. This was discovered by those investors who bought steel shares in 1960 thinking that the high earnings yields offered plenty of safety against a deterioration in the industry's profits. But in 1962 this earnings cover disappeared and some of the companies cut their dividends.

APPENDIX B

Further Reading

GENERAL

The Great Crash by J. K. Galbraith (Pelican, 3s. 6d.).
  Compulsory reading for all those intending to invest. It is the
  only antidote to the higher lunacies of a strong bull market.

How the City Works by Sir Oscar Hobson (News Chronicle,
  7s. 6d.).
  Old, but still immensely worthwhile. An introduction to the
  whole of the City—not merely the Stock Exchange.

The City by Paul Ferris (Gollancz, 21s.).
  Immensely readable, very gossipy and penetrating outsider's
  view of the City—particularly the Stock Exchange, the
  Merchant Banks and the Money Market.

Bid for Power by George Bull & Anthony Vice (Elek, 35s.).
  The real story of the take-over battles of the past decade. It
  also contains a useful "do-it-yourself" take-over chapter as
  well as advice to shareholders being taken over.

PARTICULAR

Beginners Please by the Investors Chronicle (Eyre & Spottis-
  woode, 30s.).
  Without a doubt the best all-round reference book on the
  stock market. It contains *everything*.

An Investors Guide by the Financial Times (Financial Times,
  15s.).
  An introduction to developing an investment policy
  containing three excellent chapters on analysing balance
  sheets.

Investment Arithmetic by M. S. Rix (Pitman, 20s.).

Exactly what the name implies—all the arithmetical calculations that you will come across in investment and what they are and what they do.

Balance Sheets by Philip Tovey; revised by F. Clive de Paula (Pitman, 12s. 6d.).

An excellent textbook on balance sheets and a good complement to *Investment Arithmetic*.

APPENDIX C

Stock Exchange Commissions

The Commission on share transactions is $1\frac{1}{4}\%$ on the consideration money. However, there are certain exceptions in the cost of small and large bargains.

SMALL BARGINS

No lower Commission than £2 may be charged except in the case of:

(a) transactions on which the commission may be at discretion;

(b) transactions amounting to less than £100 in value on which a commission of not less than £1 must be charged;

(c) transactions amounting to less than £10 in value on which the commission may be at discretion.

£5,000 RULE

In the case of a transaction in which the consideration exceeds £5,000, full commission must be charged up to the full amount, but a broker may at his discretion charge a reduced commission on the balance at not less than half the standard rate.

APPENDIX D

Transfer Stamp Duties

						£	s.	d.
Any Registered Stocks and Shares (subject to stamp duty) where the amount or value of the consideration for the sale does not exceed £1 5s.						0	0	3

Exceeds

						£	s.	d.
£1 5s. but does not exceed £2 10s.						0	0	6
£2 10s.	,,	,,	,,	,,	£3 15s.	0	0	9
£3 15s.	,,	,,	,,	,,	£5	0	1	0
£5	,,	,,	,,	,,	£10	0	2	0
£10	,,	,,	,,	,,	£15	0	3	0
£15	,,	,,	,,	,,	£20	0	4	0
£20	,,	,,	,,	,,	£35	0	5	0
£35	,,	,,	,,	,,	£60	0	10	0
£60	,,	,,	,,	,,	£80	0	15	0
£80	,,	,,	,,	,,	£100	1	0	0
£100	,,	,,	,,	,,	£125	1	5	0
£125	,,	,,	,,	,,	£150	1	10	0
£150	,,	,,	,,	,,	£175	1	15	0
£175	,,	,,	,,	,,	£200	2	0	0
£200	,,	,,	,,	,,	£225	2	5	0
£225	,,	,,	,,	,,	£250	2	10	0
£250	,,	,,	,,	,,	£275	5	15	0
£275	,,	,,	,,	,,	£300	3	0	0
£300—for every £50 and also for any fractional part of £50						1	10	0

Contract Stamps

	£	s.	d.
Where the value of the transaction is £5 and does not exceed £100	0	1	0
Exceeds: £100 and does not exceed £500	0	2	0

						£	s	d
£500	,,	,,	.,	,,	£1,000	0	4	0
£1,000	,,	,,	,,	,,	£1,500	0	6	0
£1,500	,,	,,	,,	,,	£2,500	0	8	0
£2,500	,,	,,	,,	,,	£5,000	0	12	0
£5,000	,,	,,	,,	,,	£7,500	0	16	0
£7,500	,,	,,	,,	,,	£10,000	1	0	0
£10,000	,,	,,	,,	,,	£12,500	1	4	0
£12,500	,,	,,	,,	,,	£15,000	1	8	0
£15,000	,,	,,	,.	,,	£17,500	1	12	0
£17,500	,,	,,	,,	,,	£20,000	1	16	0
£20,000 and over						2	0	0

Index

125